2005 SUPPLEMENT

CONSTITUTIONAL LAW

FIFTEENTH EDITION

by

KATHLEEN M. SULLIVAN
Stanley Morrison Professor of Law and
Former Dean of the School of Law,
Stanford University

GERALD GUNTHER
Late William Nelson Cromwell Professor of Law Emeritus,
Stanford University

FOUNDATION PRESS

NEW YORK, NEW YORK

2005

© 2005 By FOUNDATION PRESS

       395 Hudson Street

       New York, NY 10014

       Phone Toll Free 1–877–888–1330

       Fax (212) 367–6799

       fdpress.com

Printed in the United States of America

ISBN 1–58778–703–2

 *TEXT IS PRINTED ON 10% POST CONSUMER RECYCLED PAPER*

TABLE OF CONTENTS

Page numbers on the left indicate where the new cases fit into the casebook. Principal cases are in **bold face**.

TABLE OF CASES

Principal cases are in bold type. Non-principal cases are in roman type. References are to Pages.

*

TABLE OF AUTHORITIES

*

2005 SUPPLEMENT

CONSTITUTIONAL LAW

*

CHAPTER 3

THE COMMERCE POWER

Page 178.   Add after United States v. Morrison:

Gonzales v. Raich

___ U.S. ___, 125 S.Ct. 2195 (2005).

Justice STEVENS delivered the opinion of the court [in which Justices KENNEDY, SOUTER, GINSBURG, and BREYER joined].

California is one of at least nine States that authorize the use of marijuana for medicinal purposes. The question presented in this case is whether the power vested in Congress by Article I, § 8, of the Constitution "to make all Laws which shall be necessary and proper for carrying into Execution" its authority to "regulate Commerce with foreign Nations, and among the several States" includes the power to prohibit the local cultivation and use of marijuana in compliance with California law.

I.   California has been a pioneer in the regulation of marijuana. In 1913, California was one of the first States to prohibit the sale and possession of marijuana, and at the end of the century, California became the first State to authorize limited use of the drug for medicinal purposes. In 1996, California voters passed Proposition 215, now codified as the Compassionate Use Act of 1996. The proposition was designed to ensure that "seriously ill" residents of the State have access to marijuana for medical purposes, and to encourage Federal and State Governments to take steps towards ensuring the safe and affordable distribution of the drug to patients in need. The Act creates an exemption from criminal prosecution for physicians, as well as for patients and primary caregivers who possess or cultivate marijuana for medicinal purposes with the recommendation or approval of a physician.

Respondents Angel Raich and Diane Monson are California residents who suffer from a variety of serious medical conditions and have sought to avail themselves of medical marijuana pursuant to the terms of the Compassionate Use Act. [On] August 15, 2002, county deputy sheriffs and agents from the federal Drug Enforcement Administration (DEA) came to Monson's home. After a thorough investigation, the county officials concluded that her use of marijuana was entirely lawful as a matter of California law. Nevertheless, after a 3–hour standoff, the federal agents seized and destroyed all six of her cannabis plants. Respondents thereafter brought this action against the Attorney General of the United States and the head of the DEA seeking injunctive and declaratory relief prohibiting the enforcement of the federal Controlled

Substances Act (CSA), to the extent it prevents them from possessing, obtaining, or manufacturing cannabis for their personal medical use.

[The] case is made difficult by respondents' strong arguments that they will suffer irreparable harm because, despite a congressional finding to the contrary, marijuana does have valid therapeutic purposes. The question before us, however, is not whether it is wise to enforce the statute in these circumstances; rather, it is whether Congress' power to regulate interstate markets for medicinal substances encompasses the portions of those markets that are supplied with drugs produced and consumed locally. Well-settled law controls our answer. The CSA is a valid exercise of federal power.

II.   Shortly after taking office in 1969, President Nixon declared a national "war on drugs." [culminating] in the passage of the Comprehensive Drug Abuse Prevention and Control Act of 1970. [Title II] of that Act, the CSA, repealed most of the earlier antidrug laws in favor of a comprehensive regime to combat the international and interstate traffic in illicit drugs. The main objectives of the CSA were to conquer drug abuse and to control the legitimate and illegitimate traffic in controlled substances. Congress was particularly concerned with the need to prevent the diversion of drugs from legitimate to illicit channels. [In] enacting the CSA, Congress classified marijuana as a Schedule I drug. [Schedule I] drugs are categorized as such because of their high potential for abuse, lack of any accepted medical use, and absence of any accepted safety for use in medically supervised treatment. [By] classifying marijuana as a Schedule I drug, the manufacture, distribution, or possession of marijuana became a criminal offense.

III.   Respondents in this case do not dispute that passage of the CSA [was] well within Congress' commerce power. Nor do they contend that any provision or section of the CSA amounts to an unconstitutional exercise of congressional authority. Rather, [they] argue that the CSA's categorical prohibition of the manufacture and possession of marijuana as applied to the intrastate manufacture and possession of marijuana for medical purposes pursuant to California law exceeds Congress' authority under the Commerce Clause.

[Our] case law firmly establishes Congress' power to regulate purely local activities that are part of an economic "class of activities" that have a substantial effect on interstate commerce. Perez (1971) [15th ed., p. 153]; Wickard v. Filburn (1942) [15th ed., p. 147]. [Our] decision in Wickard is of particular relevance. In Wickard, we upheld the application of regulations promulgated under the Agricultural Adjustment Act of 1938 which were designed to control the volume of wheat moving in interstate and foreign commerce in order to avoid surpluses and consequent abnormally low prices. The regulations established an allotment of 11.1 acres for Filburn's 1941 wheat crop, but he sowed 23 acres, intending to use the excess by consuming it on his own farm. Filburn argued that even though we had sustained Congress' power to regulate the production of goods for commerce, that power did not authorize "federal regulation [of] production not intended in any part for commerce but wholly for consumption on the farm." Justice Jackson's opinion for a unanimous Court rejected this submission. [Wickard] thus establishes that Congress can regulate purely intrastate activity that is not itself "commercial," in that it is not produced for sale, if it concludes that failure to regulate that class of activity would undercut the regulation of the interstate market in that commodity.

The similarities between this case and Wickard are striking. Like the farmer in Wickard, respondents are cultivating, for home consumption, a fungible commodity for which there is an established, albeit illegal, interstate market. Just as the Agricultural Adjustment Act was designed "to control the volume [of wheat] moving in interstate and foreign commerce in order to avoid surpluses . . ." and consequently control the market price, a primary purpose of the CSA is to control the supply and demand of controlled substances in both lawful and unlawful drug markets. In Wickard, we had no difficulty concluding that Congress had a rational basis for believing that, when viewed in the aggregate, leaving home-consumed wheat outside the regulatory scheme would have a substantial influence on price and market conditions. Here too, Congress had a rational basis for concluding that leaving home-consumed marijuana outside federal control would similarly affect price and market conditions. [In] both cases, the regulation is squarely within Congress' commerce power because production of the commodity meant for home consumption, be it wheat or marijuana, has a substantial effect on supply and demand in the national market for that commodity.

Nonetheless, respondents suggest that Wickard differs from this case in three respects: (1) the Agricultural Adjustment Act, unlike the CSA, exempted small farming operations; (2) Wickard involved a "quintessential economic activity"—a commercial farm—whereas respondents do not sell marijuana; and (3) the Wickard record made it clear that the aggregate production of wheat for use on farms had a significant impact on market prices. Those differences, though factually accurate, do not diminish the precedential force of this Court's reasoning.

The fact that Wickard's own impact on the market was "trivial by itself" was not a sufficient reason for removing him from the scope of federal regulation. [And] while it is true that the record in the Wickard case itself established the causal connection between the production for local use and the national market, we have before us findings by Congress to the same effect. [True,] Congress did not make a specific finding that the intrastate cultivation and possession of marijuana for medical purposes based on the recommendation of a physician would substantially affect the larger interstate marijuana market. [But] we have never required Congress to make particularized findings in order to legislate. [While] we will consider congressional findings in our analysis when they are available, the absence of particularized findings does not call into question Congress' authority to legislate.

In assessing the scope of Congress' authority under the Commerce Clause, we stress that the task before us is a modest one. We need not determine whether respondents' activities, taken in the aggregate, substantially affect interstate commerce in fact, but only whether a "rational basis" exists for so concluding. Given the enforcement difficulties that attend distinguishing between marijuana cultivated locally and marijuana grown elsewhere, and concerns about diversion into illicit channels, we have no difficulty concluding that Congress had a rational basis for believing that failure to regulate the intrastate manufacture and possession of marijuana would leave a gaping hole in the CSA. Thus, as in Wickard, when it enacted comprehensive legislation to regulate the interstate market in a fungible commodity, Congress was acting well within its authority to "make all Laws which shall be necessary and proper" to "regulate Commerce ... among the several States." U.S. Const., Art. I, § 8. That the regulation ensnares some purely intrastate activity is of no moment. As we have done many times before, we refuse to excise individual components of that larger scheme.

IV.   To support their contrary submission, respondents rely heavily on two of our more recent Commerce Clause cases. [They] read those cases far too broadly. Those two cases, of course, are Lopez (1995) [15th ed., p. 153] and Morrison (2000) [15th ed., p. 173]. [Here,] respondents ask us to excise individual applications of a concededly valid statutory scheme. In contrast, in both Lopez and Morrison, the parties asserted that a particular statute or provision fell outside Congress' commerce power in its entirety. This distinction is pivotal.

[At] issue in Lopez was the validity of the Gun–Free School Zones Act of 1990, which was a brief, single-subject statute making it a crime for an individual to possess a gun in a school zone. The Act did not regulate any economic activity and did not contain any requirement that the possession of a gun have any connection to past interstate activity or a predictable impact on future commercial activity. [The] statutory scheme that the Government is defending in this litigation is at the opposite end of the regulatory spectrum. [The] CSA [was] a lengthy and detailed statute creating a comprehensive framework for regulating the production, distribution, and possession of five classes of "controlled substances." [Classification of marijuana as a controlled substance,] unlike the discrete prohibition established by the Gun–Free School Zones Act of 1990, was merely one of many "essential parts of a larger regulation of economic activity, in which the regulatory scheme could be undercut unless the intrastate activity were regulated." Our opinion in Lopez casts no doubt on the validity of such a program.

Nor does this Court's holding in Morrison. The Violence Against Women Act of 1994 created a federal civil remedy for the victims of gender-motivated crimes of violence. [Despite] congressional findings that such crimes had an adverse impact on interstate commerce, we held the statute unconstitutional because, like the statute in Lopez, it did not regulate economic activity. [Unlike] those at issue in Lopez and Morrison, the activities regulated by the CSA are quintessentially economic. [The] CSA is a statute that regulates the production, distribution, and consumption of commodities for which there is an established, and lucrative, interstate market. Prohibiting the intrastate possession or manufacture of an article of commerce is a rational (and commonly utilized) means of regulating commerce in that product. [Because] the CSA is a statute that directly regulates economic, commercial activity, our opinion in Morrison casts no doubt on its constitutionality.

[If,] as [Justice O'Connor's dissent] contends, the personal cultivation, possession, and use of marijuana for medicinal purposes is beyond the " 'outer limits' of Congress' Commerce Clause authority," it must also be true that such personal use of marijuana (or any other homegrown drug) for recreational purposes is also beyond those " 'outer limits,' " whether or not a State elects to authorize or even regulate such use. [One] need not have a degree in economics to understand why a nationwide exemption for the vast quantity of marijuana (or other drugs) locally cultivated for personal use (which presumably would include use by friends, neighbors, and family members) may have a substantial impact on the interstate market for this extraordinarily popular substance. [The] exemption for physicians provides them with an economic incentive to grant their patients permission to use the drug. [The] exemption for cultivation by patients and caregivers can only increase the supply of marijuana in the California market. The likelihood that all such production will promptly terminate when patients recover or will precisely match the patients' medical needs during their convalescence seems remote; whereas the danger that excesses will satisfy some of the admittedly enormous demand for recreational use seems obvious. Moreover, that the national and international narcotics trade has thrived in the face of vigorous criminal enforcement efforts suggests that no small number of unscrupulous people will make use of the California exemptions to serve their commercial ends whenever it is feasible to do so. Taking into account the fact that California is only one of at least nine States to have authorized the medical use of marijuana, [Congress] could have rationally concluded that the aggregate impact on the national market of all the transactions exempted from federal supervision is unquestionably substantial.

[The] case for the exemption comes down to the claim that a locally cultivated product that is used domestically rather than sold on the open market is not subject to federal regulation. Given the findings in the CSA and the undisputed magnitude of the commercial market for marijuana, our decisions in Wickard v. Filburn and the later cases endorsing its reasoning foreclose that claim.

V.   Respondents also raise a substantive due process claim and seek to avail themselves of the medical necessity defense. [We] do not address the question whether judicial relief is available to respondents on these alternative bases.

[Vacated and remanded.]

Justice SCALIA, concurring in the judgment.

I agree with the Court's holding that the Controlled Substances Act (CSA) may validly be applied to respondents' cultivation, distribution, and possession of marijuana for personal, medicinal use. I write separately because my understanding of the doctrinal foundation on which that holding rests is, if not inconsistent with that of the Court, at least more nuanced.

[Unlike] the channels, instrumentalities, and agents of interstate commerce, activities that substantially affect interstate commerce are not themselves part of interstate commerce, and thus the power to regulate them cannot come from the Commerce Clause alone. Rather, Congress's regulatory authority over [such] activities [derives] from the Necessary and Proper Clause. [The] authority to enact laws necessary and proper for the regulation of interstate commerce is not limited to laws governing intrastate activities that substantially affect interstate commerce. Where necessary to make a regulation of interstate commerce effective, Congress may regulate even those intrastate activities that do not themselves substantially affect interstate commerce.

I.   Our cases show that the regulation of intrastate activities may be necessary to and proper for the regulation of interstate commerce in two general circumstances. Most directly, the commerce power permits Congress not only to devise rules for the governance of commerce between States but also to facilitate interstate commerce by eliminating potential obstructions, and to restrict it by eliminating potential stimulants. Lopez and Morrison recognized the expansive scope of Congress's authority in this regard. [This] principle is not without limitation. In Lopez and Morrison, the Court [rejected] the argument that Congress may regulate noneconomic activity based solely on the effect that it may have on interstate commerce through a remote chain of inferences. [As] we implicitly acknowledged in Lopez, however, Congress's authority to enact laws necessary and proper for the regulation of interstate commerce is not limited to laws directed against economic activities that have a substantial effect on interstate commerce. Though the conduct in Lopez was not economic, the Court nevertheless recognized that it could be regulated as "an essential part of a larger regulation of economic activity, in which the regulatory scheme could be undercut unless the intrastate activity were regulated." [The] regulation of an intrastate activity may be essential to a comprehensive regulation of interstate commerce even though the intrastate activity does not itself "substantially affect" interstate commerce. Moreover, [Congress] may regulate even noneconomic local activity if that regulation is a necessary part of a more general regulation of interstate commerce. The relevant question is simply whether the means chosen are "reasonably adapted" to the attainment of a legitimate end under the commerce power.

II. [Justice O'Connor's] dissent objects that, by permitting Congress to regulate activities necessary to effective interstate regulation, the Court reduces Lopez and Morrison to "little more than a drafting guide." I think that criticism unjustified. Unlike the power to regulate activities that have a substantial effect on interstate commerce, the power to enact laws enabling effective regulation of interstate commerce can only be exercised in conjunction with congressional regulation of an interstate market, and it extends only to those measures necessary to make the interstate regulation effective. [This] is not a power that threatens to obliterate the line between "what is truly national and what is truly local." Lopez and Morrison affirm that Congress may not regulate certain "purely local" activity within the States based solely on the attenuated effect that such activity may have in the interstate market. But those decisions do not declare noneconomic intrastate activities to be categorically beyond the reach of the Federal Government. [The] Necessary and Proper Clause [empowers] Congress to enact laws in effectuation of its enumerated powers that are not within its authority to enact in isolation. See McCulloch v. Maryland (1819) [15th ed., p. 90].

III. The application of these principles to the case before us is straightforward. In the CSA, Congress has undertaken to extinguish the interstate market in Schedule I controlled substances, including marijuana. The Commerce Clause unquestionably permits this. [To] effectuate its objective, Congress has prohibited almost all intrastate activities related to Schedule I substances—both economic activities (manufacture, distribution, possession with the intent to distribute) and noneconomic activities (simple possession). That simple possession is a noneconomic activity is immaterial to whether it can be prohibited as a necessary part of a larger regulation. [By] this measure, I think the regulation must be sustained. [Drugs] like marijuana are fungible commodities. [Marijuana] that is grown at home and possessed for personal use is never more than an instant from the interstate market. [Congress] need not accept on faith that state law will be effective in maintaining a strict division between a lawful market for "medical" marijuana and the more general marijuana market. [I] thus agree with the Court that [Congress] could reasonably conclude that its objective of prohibiting marijuana from the interstate market "could be undercut" if those activities were excepted from its general scheme of regulation.

Justice O'CONNOR, with whom Chief Justice [REHNQUIST] and Justice THOMAS join as to all but Part III, dissenting.

We enforce the "outer limits" of Congress' Commerce Clause authority not for their own sake, but to protect historic spheres of state sovereignty from excessive federal encroachment and thereby to maintain the distribution of power fundamental to our federalist system of government. One of federalism's chief virtues, of course, is that it promotes innovation by allowing for the possibility that "a single courageous State may, if its citizens choose, serve as a laboratory; and try novel social and economic experiments without risk to the rest of the country." New State Ice Co. v. Liebmann, (1932) (Brandeis, J., dissenting).

This case exemplifies the role of States as laboratories. The States' core police powers have always included authority to define criminal law and to protect the health, safety, and welfare of their citizens. Exercising those powers, California (by ballot initiative and then by legislative codification) has come to its own conclusion about the difficult and sensitive question of whether marijuana should be available to relieve severe pain and suffering. Today the Court sanctions an application of the federal Controlled Substances Act that extinguishes that experiment, without any proof that the personal cultivation, possession, and use of marijuana for medicinal purposes, if economic activity in the first place, has a substantial effect on interstate commerce and is therefore an appropriate subject of federal regulation. In so doing, the Court announces a rule that gives Congress a perverse incentive to legislate broadly pursuant to the Commerce Clause—nestling questionable assertions of its authority into comprehensive regulatory schemes—rather than with precision. That rule and the result it produces in this case are irreconcilable with our decisions in Lopez and Morrison. Accordingly I dissent.

I.   In Lopez, [our] decision about whether gun possession in school zones substantially affected interstate commerce turned on four considerations. First, we observed that our "substantial effects" cases generally have upheld federal regulation of economic activity that affected interstate commerce. [Second,] we noted that the statute contained no express jurisdictional requirement establishing its connection to interstate commerce. Third, we found telling the absence of legislative findings about the regulated conduct's impact on interstate commerce. [Finally,] we rejected as too attenuated the Government's argument that firearm possession in school zones could result in violent crime which in turn could adversely affect the national economy. [In] my view, the case before us is materially indistinguishable from Lopez and Morrison when the same considerations are taken into account.

II.   [Today's] decision suggests that the federal regulation of local activity is immune to Commerce Clause challenge because Congress chose to act with an ambitious, all-encompassing statute, rather than piecemeal. [Today's] decision allows Congress to regulate intrastate activity without check, so long as there is some implication by legislative design that regulating intrastate activity is essential (and the Court appears to equate "essential" with "necessary") to the interstate regulatory scheme. [The] Court appears to reason that the placement of local activity in a comprehensive scheme confirms that it is essential to that scheme. If the Court is right, then Lopez stands for nothing more than a drafting guide: Congress should have described the relevant crime as "transfer or possession of a firearm anywhere in the nation" [or attached] the regulation of intrastate activity to a pre-existing comprehensive (or even not-so-comprehensive) scheme. I cannot agree that our decision in Lopez contemplated such evasive or overbroad legislative strategies with approval. Until today, such arguments have been made only in dissent. [If] the Court always defers to Congress as it does today, little may be left to the notion of enumerated powers.

[The] Court's definition of economic activity is breathtaking [and] threatens to sweep all of productive human activity into federal regulatory reach. [It] will not do to say that Congress may regulate noncommercial activity simply because it may have an effect on the demand for commercial goods, or because the noncommercial endeavor can, in some sense, substitute for commercial activity. Most commercial goods or services have some sort of privately producible analogue. Home care substitutes for daycare. Charades games substitute for movie tickets. Backyard or windowsill gardening substitutes for going to the supermarket. To draw the line wherever private activity affects the demand for market goods is to draw no line at all, and to declare everything economic. We have already rejected the result that would follow—a federal police power. Lopez.

In Lopez and Morrison, we suggested that economic activity usually relates directly to commercial activity. The homegrown cultivation and personal possession and use of marijuana for medicinal purposes has no apparent commercial character. Everyone agrees that the marijuana at issue in this case was never in the stream of commerce, and neither were the supplies for growing it. (Marijuana is highly unusual among the substances subject to the CSA in that it can be cultivated without any materials that have traveled in interstate commerce.) Lopez makes clear that possession is not itself commercial activity. And respondents have not come into possession by means of any commercial transaction; they have simply grown, in their own homes, marijuana for their own use, without acquiring, buying, selling, or bartering a thing of value.

The Court suggests that Wickard, which we have identified as "perhaps the most far reaching example of Commerce Clause authority over intrastate activity," established federal regulatory power over any home consumption of a commodity for which a national market exists. I disagree. [In] contrast to the CSA's limitless assertion of power, Congress provided an exemption within the AAA for small producers. When Filburn planted the wheat at issue in Wickard, the statute exempted plantings less than 200 bushels (about six tons), and when he harvested his wheat it exempted plantings less than six acres. Wickard, then, did not extend Commerce Clause authority to something as modest as the home cook's herb garden. [Wickard] did not hold or imply that small-scale production of commodities is always economic, and automatically within Congress' reach.

Even assuming that economic activity is at issue in this case, the Government has made no showing in fact that the possession and use of homegrown marijuana for medical purposes, in California or elsewhere, has a substantial effect on interstate commerce. Similarly, the Government has not shown that regulating such activity is necessary to an interstate regulatory scheme. Whatever the specific theory of "substantial effects" at issue (i.e., whether the activity substantially affects interstate commerce, whether its regulation is necessary to an interstate regulatory scheme, or both), a concern for dual sovereignty requires that Congress' excursion into the traditional domain of States be justified.

There is simply no evidence that homegrown medicinal marijuana users constitute, in the aggregate, a sizable enough class to have a discernable, let alone substantial, impact on the national illicit drug market—or otherwise to threaten the CSA regime. [Common] sense suggests that medical marijuana users may be limited in number and that California's Compassionate Use Act and similar state legislation may well isolate activities relating to medicinal marijuana from the illicit market. In [Wickard,] the Court was able to consider "actual effects" because the parties had "stipulated a summary of the economics of the wheat industry." [The CSA's] bare declarations cannot be compared to the record before the Court in Wickard. They amount to nothing more than a legislative insistence that the regulation of controlled substances must be absolute. They are asserted without any supporting evidence—descriptive, statistical, or otherwise. [Indeed,] if declarations like these suffice to justify federal regulation, and if the Court today is right about what passes rationality review before us, then our decision in Morrison should have come out the other way. In that case, Congress had supplied numerous findings regarding the impact gender-motivated violence had on the national economy. If, as the Court claims, today's decision does not break with precedent, how can it be that voluminous findings, documenting extensive hearings about the specific topic of violence against women, did not pass constitutional muster in Morrison, while the CSA's abstract, unsubstantiated, generalized findings about controlled substances do?

III. [We] would do well to recall how James Madison, the father of the Constitution, described our system of joint sovereignty to the people of New York: "The powers delegated by the proposed constitution to the federal government are few and defined. Those which are to remain in the State governments are numerous and indefinite.... The powers reserved to the several States will extend to all the objects which, in the ordinary course of affairs, concern the lives, liberties, and properties of the people, and the internal order, improvement, and prosperity of the State." The Federalist No. 45, pp. 292–293 (C. Rossiter ed. 1961).

Relying on Congress' abstract assertions, the Court has endorsed making it a federal crime to grow small amounts of marijuana in one's own home for one's own medicinal use. This overreaching stifles an express choice by some States, concerned for the lives and liberties of their people, to regulate medical marijuana differently. If I were a California citizen, I would not have voted for the medical marijuana ballot initiative; if I were a California legislator I would not have supported the Compassionate Use Act. But whatever the wisdom of California's experiment with medical marijuana, the federalism principles that have driven our Commerce Clause cases require that room for experiment be protected in this case. For these reasons I dissent.

Justice THOMAS, dissenting.

Respondents Diane Monson and Angel Raich use marijuana that has never been bought or sold, that has never crossed state lines, and that has had no demonstrable effect on the national market for marijuana. If Congress can regulate this under the Commerce Clause, then it can regulate virtually anything—and the Federal Government is no longer one of limited and enumerated powers.

Respondents' local cultivation and consumption of marijuana is not "Commerce . . . among the several States." U.S. Const., Art. I, § 8, cl. 3. [The] Commerce Clause empowers Congress to regulate the buying and selling of goods and services trafficked across state lines. The Clause's text, structure, and history all indicate that, at the time of the founding, the term " 'commerce' consisted of selling, buying, and bartering, as well as transporting for these purposes." [No] evidence from the founding suggests that "commerce" included the mere possession of a good or some purely personal activity that did not involve trade or exchange for value. In the early days of the Republic, it would have been unthinkable that Congress could prohibit the local cultivation, possession, and consumption of marijuana.

[The] CSA, as applied to respondents' conduct, is not a valid exercise of Congress' power under the Necessary and Proper Clause. [The] question is [whether] the intrastate ban is "necessary and proper" as applied to medical marijuana users like respondents. Respondents are not regulable simply because they belong to a large class (local growers and users of marijuana) that Congress might need to reach, if they also belong to a distinct and separable subclass (local growers and users of state-authorized, medical marijuana) that does not undermine the CSA's interstate ban. [We] normally presume that States enforce their own laws. [Nothing] suggests that California's controls are ineffective. The scant evidence that exists suggests that few people—the vast majority of whom are aged 40 or older—register to use medical marijuana. In part because of the low incidence of medical marijuana use, many law enforcement officials report that the introduction of medical marijuana laws has not affected their law enforcement efforts. [These] controls belie the Government's assertion that placing medical marijuana outside the CSA's reach "would prevent effective enforcement of the interstate ban on drug trafficking."

Even assuming the CSA's ban on locally cultivated and consumed marijuana is "necessary," that does not mean it is also "proper." [Congress] may not use its incidental authority to subvert basic principles of federalism and dual sovereignty. Here, Congress has encroached on States' traditional police powers to define the criminal law and to protect the health, safety, and welfare of their citizens. [The] majority defines economic activity in the broadest possible terms. [If] the majority is to be taken seriously, the Federal Government may now regulate quilting bees, clothes drives, and potluck suppers throughout the 50 States. This makes a mockery of Madison's assurance to the people of New York that the "powers delegated" to the Federal Government are "few and defined, while those of the States are" numerous and indefinite. The Federalist No. 45.

[The] majority prevents States like California from devising drug policies that they have concluded provide much-needed respite to the seriously ill. It does so without any serious inquiry into the necessity for federal regulation or the propriety of "displacing state regulation in areas of traditional state concern." [Our] federalist system, properly understood, allows California and a growing number of other States to decide for themselves how to safeguard the health and welfare of their citizens. [I] respectfully dissent.

CHAPTER 5

FEDERAL LIMITS ON STATE POWER TO REGULATE THE NATIONAL ECONOMY

SECTION 1. STATE REGULATION AND THE DORMANT COMMERCE CLAUSE

Page 269. Add after Note 5:

6. *Facially discriminatory state laws and the 21st Amendment.* Does the antidiscrimination principle of the dormant Commerce Clause prevail even over a unique provision of the Constitution that accords states some explicit power over interstate commerce? Section 2 of the Twenty-first Amendment, enacted in 1933 as part of the repeal of national Prohibition, provides: "The transportation or importation into any State, Territory, or possession of the United States for delivery or use therein of intoxicating liquors, in violation of the laws thereof, is hereby prohibited."

Some state liquor authorities construed section 2 broadly, contending that, with respect to alcoholic beverages, even laws that expressly favored local producers over out-of-state producers should be immune from or readily satisfy dormant commerce clause scrutiny.

An unusual 5–4 majority of the Court squarely rejected that argument in GRANHOLM v. HEALD, ___ U.S. ___, 125 S.Ct. 1885 (2005), a consolidated set of cases arising from challenges by out-of-state wineries and in-state consumers to Michigan and New York laws that provided that in-state wineries could ship wine directly to consumers, but out-of-state wineries could not. Justice KENNEDY, joined by Justices Scalia, Souter, Ginsburg and Breyer wrote the opinion of the Court: "We hold that the laws in both States discriminate against interstate commerce in violation of the Commerce Clause, Art. I, § 8, cl. 3, and that the discrimination is neither authorized nor permitted by the Twenty-first Amendment. [The] differential treatment between in-state and out-of-state wineries constitutes explicit discrimination against interstate commerce. [Time] and again this Court has held that, in all but the narrowest circumstances, state laws violate the Commerce Clause if they mandate 'differential treatment of in-state and out-of-state economic interests that benefits the former and burdens the latter.' This rule is essential to the foundations of the Union. The mere fact of nonresidence should not foreclose a producer in one State from access to markets in other States. [Laws] of the type at issue in the instant cases contradict these principles. They deprive citizens of their right to have access to the markets of other States on equal terms. The perceived necessity for reciprocal sale privileges risks generating the trade rivalries and animosities, the alliances and exclusivity, that the Constitution and, in particular, the Commerce Clause were designed to avoid. State laws that protect local wineries have led to the enactment of statutes under which some States condition the right of out-of-state wineries to make direct wine sales to in-state consumers on a reciprocal right in the shipping State. [The] current patchwork of laws—with some States banning direct shipments altogether, others doing so only for out-of-state wines, and still others requiring reciprocity—is essentially the product of an ongoing, low-level trade war.

"We have no difficulty concluding that New York, like Michigan, discriminates against interstate commerce through its direct-shipping laws. State laws that discriminate against interstate commerce face 'a virtually *per se* rule of invalidity.' Philadelphia v. New Jersey (1978) [15th ed., p. 257]. The Michigan and New York laws by their own terms violate this proscription. The two States, however, contend their statutes are saved by § 2 of the Twenty-first Amendment. [The] States' position is inconsistent with our precedents and with the Twenty-first Amendment's history. Section 2 does not allow States to regulate the direct shipment of wine on terms that discriminate in favor of in-state producers." Justice Kennedy reviewed the history of commerce clause challenges to state liquor regulations both before and after Prohibition and its repeal, and concluded that, while states might regulate liquor imports in order to reinforce domestic liquor regulation, and prevent bootlegging at their borders from undermining local temperance should they choose to adopt it, "States were required to regulate domestic and imported liquor on equal terms. [The] aim of the Twenty-first Amendment was to allow States to maintain an effective and uniform system for controlling liquor by regulating its transportation, importation, and use. The Amendment did not give States the authority to pass nonuniform laws in order to discriminate against out-of-state goods, a privilege they had not enjoyed at any earlier time."

Justice Kennedy conceded that some decisions of the Court shortly after passage of the Twenty-first Amendment "were inconsistent with this view," but emphasized that "more recent cases [confirm] that the Twenty-first Amendment does not supersede other provisions of the Constitution and, in particular, does not displace the rule that States may not give a discriminatory preference to their own producers." Noting that the Court had struck down state regulations of alcoholic beverage sales that violated other provisions of the Constitution, including the First Amendment, the Equal Protection Clause, and the Establishment Clause, he concluded that a law violating the structural principle of federal union reflected in the dormant Commerce Clause likewise was not saved by the Twenty-first Amendment. He reaffirmed the Court's 1984 holding in Bacchus Imports v. Dias [15th ed., p. 278], over the states' efforts to distinguish or overrule it: "The Court has held that state regulation of alcohol is limited by the nondiscrimination principle of the Commerce Clause. Bacchus provides a particularly telling example of this proposition. At issue was an excise tax enacted by Hawaii that exempted certain alcoholic beverages produced in that State. The Court rejected the argument that Hawaii's discrimination against out-of-state liquor was authorized by the Twenty-first Amendment. 'The central purpose of the [Amendment] was not to empower States to favor local liquor industries by erecting barriers to competition.' "

Applying strict scrutiny to the New York and Michigan laws, Justice Kennedy found that neither the state interest in preventing underage drinking nor in collecting tax revenues could justify *discriminatory* wine shipping laws: "Even were we to credit the States' largely unsupported claim that direct shipping of wine increases the risk of underage drinking, this would not justify regulations limiting only out-of-state direct shipments. As the wineries point out, minors are just as likely to order wine from in-state producers as from out-of-state ones. [In] addition, the States can take less restrictive steps to minimize the risk that minors will order wine by mail. For example, the Model Direct Shipping Bill developed by the National Conference of State Legislatures requires an adult signature on delivery and a label so instructing on each package. [The] States' tax-collection justification is also insufficient. Increased direct shipping, whether originating in state or out of state, brings with it the potential for tax evasion. [A state] could protect itself against lost tax revenue by requiring a permit as a condition of direct shipping. The States have not shown that tax evasion from out-of-state wineries poses such a unique threat that it justifies their discriminatory regimes. [Our] Commerce Clause cases demand more than mere speculation to support discrimination against out-of-state goods."

Justice THOMAS wrote a lengthy dissent, joined by Chief Justice Rehnquist and Justices Stevens and O'Connor. While Justice Thomas has continued in other cases to take the view that the negative Commerce Clause has no basis in the text of the Constitution, and is not a proper basis for invalidating state laws, see, e.g., American Trucking Assn. v. Michigan Public Service Comm., 545 U.S. ___, 125 S.Ct. 2419 (2005) (Thomas, J., concurring in the Court's unanimous judgment that a flat fee on trucks engaged in intrastate hauling did not violate the dormant Commerce Clause as applied to truckers engaged predominantly in interstate commerce), he did not rest his dissent in Granholm v. Heald upon such a basis. Rather, he read the discriminatory New York and Michigan laws as affirmatively authorized by Congress in the Webb–Kenyon Act of 1913, and thus immune from dormant Commerce Clause scrutiny, or alternatively as authorized by the Twenty-first Amendment. Justice STEVENS wrote a separate dissent adverting to his own experience as the Court's eldest member: "My understanding (and recollection) of the historical context reinforces my conviction that the text of § 2 should be 'broadly and colloquially interpreted.'"

CHAPTER 8

SUBSTANTIVE DUE PROCESS: RISE, DECLINE, REVIVAL

SECTION 2. CONSTITUTIONAL SAFEGUARDS OF ECONOMIC RIGHTS: THE TAKINGS CLAUSE; THE CONTRACTS CLAUSE

Page 516. Add after Hawaii Housing Authority v. Midkiff:

Kelo v. City of New London

___ U.S. ___, 125 S.Ct. 2655 (2005).

Justice STEVENS delivered the opinion of the Court [in which Justices KENNEDY, SOUTER, GINSBURG, and BREYER joined].

In 2000, the city of New London approved a development plan that [was] "projected to create in excess of 1,000 jobs, to increase tax and other revenues, and to revitalize an economically distressed city, including its downtown and waterfront areas." In assembling the land needed for this project, the city's development agent has purchased property from willing sellers and proposes to use the power of eminent domain to acquire the remainder of the property from unwilling owners in exchange for just compensation. The question presented is whether the city's proposed disposition of this property qualifies as a "public use" within the meaning of the Takings Clause of the Fifth Amendment to the Constitution.

I. The city of New London [suffered] decades of economic decline [that] led a state agency in 1990 to designate the City a "distressed municipality." [In] 1998, the City's unemployment rate was nearly double that of the State, and its population of just under 24,000 residents was at its lowest since 1920. These conditions prompted state and local officials to target New London, and particularly its Fort Trumbull area, for economic revitalization. To this end, respondent New London Development Corporation (NLDC), a private nonprofit entity established some years earlier to assist the City in planning economic development, was reactivated. [The] State authorized a $5.35 million bond issue to support the NLDC's planning activities and a $10 million bond issue toward the creation of a Fort Trumbull State Park. [The] pharmaceutical company Pfizer Inc. announced that it would build a $300 million research facility on a site immediately adjacent to Fort Trumbull; local planners hoped that Pfizer would draw new business to the area, thereby serving as a catalyst to the area's rejuvenation.

II. [Petitioner] Susette Kelo has lived in the Fort Trumbull area since 1997. She has made extensive improvements to her house, which she prizes for

15

its water view. Petitioner Wilhelmina Dery was born in her Fort Trumbull house in 1918 and has lived there her entire life. [In] all, the nine petitioners own 15 properties in Fort Trumbull. [There] is no allegation that any of these properties is blighted or otherwise in poor condition; rather, they were condemned only because they happen to be located in the development area. [The] Supreme Court of Connecticut [held] that all of the City's proposed takings were valid.

III. Two polar propositions are perfectly clear. On the one hand, it has long been accepted that the sovereign may not take the property of A for the sole purpose of transferring it to another private party B, even though A is paid just compensation. On the other hand, it is equally clear that a State may transfer property from one private party to another if future "use by the public" is the purpose of the taking; the condemnation of land for a railroad with common-carrier duties is a familiar example. Neither of these propositions, however, determines the disposition of this case. [There] was no evidence of an illegitimate purpose in this case. [The] City's development plan was not adopted "to benefit a particular class of identifiable individuals." On the other hand, this is not a case in which the City is planning to open the condemned land—at least not in its entirety—to use by the general public. Nor will the private lessees of the land in any sense be required to operate like common carriers, making their services available to all comers.

But [this] "Court long ago rejected any literal requirement that condemned property be put into use for the general public." Indeed, while many state courts in the mid–19th century endorsed "use by the public" as the proper definition of public use, that narrow view steadily eroded over time. [When] this Court began applying the Fifth Amendment to the States at the close of the 19th century, it embraced the broader and more natural interpretation of public use as "public purpose." Thus, in a case upholding a mining company's use of an aerial bucket line to transport ore over property it did not own, Justice Holmes' opinion for the Court stressed "the inadequacy of use by the general public as a universal test." Strickley v. Highland Boy Gold Mining Co., 200 U.S. 527 (1906). We have repeatedly and consistently rejected that narrow test ever since.

The disposition of this case therefore turns on the question whether the City's development plan serves a "public purpose." Without exception, our cases have defined that concept broadly, reflecting our longstanding policy of deference to legislative judgments in this field. In Berman v. Parker, this Court upheld a redevelopment plan targeting a blighted area of Washington, D.C., in which most of the housing for the area's 5,000 inhabitants was beyond repair. [The] owner of a department store located in the area challenged the condemnation, pointing out that his store was not itself blighted. [Writing] for a unanimous Court, Justice Douglas refused to evaluate this claim in isolation, deferring instead to the legislative and agency judgment that the area "must be planned as a whole" for the plan to be successful. In Hawaii Housing Authority v. Midkiff, the Court considered a Hawaii statute whereby fee title was taken from lessors and transferred to lessees (for just compensation) in order to reduce the concentration of land ownership. We unanimously upheld the statute and rejected the Ninth Circuit's view that it was "a naked attempt on the part of the state of Hawaii to take the property of A and transfer it to B solely for B's private use and benefit." Reaffirming Berman's deferential approach to legislative judgments in this field, we concluded that the State's purpose of eliminating the "social and economic evils of a land oligopoly" qualified as a valid public use. [Our] public use jurisprudence has wisely eschewed rigid formulas and intrusive scrutiny in favor of affording legislatures broad latitude in determining what public needs justify the use of the takings power.

IV.   Those who govern the City were not confronted with the need to remove blight in the Fort Trumbull area, but their determination that the area was sufficiently distressed to justify a program of economic rejuvenation is entitled to our deference. The City has carefully formulated an economic development plan that it believes will provide appreciable benefits to the community, including—but by no means limited to—new jobs and increased tax revenue. [Given] the comprehensive character of the plan, the thorough deliberation that preceded its adoption, and the limited scope of our review, it is appropriate for us, as it was in Berman, to resolve the challenges of the individual owners, not on a piecemeal basis, but rather in light of the entire plan. Because that plan unquestionably serves a public purpose, the takings challenged here satisfy the public use requirement of the Fifth Amendment.

To avoid this result, petitioners urge us to adopt a new bright-line rule that economic development does not qualify as a public use. [Neither] precedent nor logic supports petitioners' proposal. Promoting economic development is a traditional and long accepted function of government. There is, moreover, no principled way of distinguishing economic development from the other public purposes that we have recognized. [Petitioners also] contend that using eminent domain for economic development impermissibly blurs the boundary between public and private takings. Again, our cases foreclose this objection. Quite simply, the government's pursuit of a public purpose will often benefit individual private parties. For example, in Midkiff, the forced transfer of property conferred a direct and significant benefit on those lessees who were previously unable to purchase their homes. [It] is further argued that without a bright-line rule nothing would stop a city from transferring citizen A's property to citizen B for the sole reason that citizen B will put the property to a more productive use and thus pay more taxes. Such a one-to-one transfer of property, executed outside the confines of an integrated development plan, is not presented in this case. While such an unusual exercise of government power would certainly raise a suspicion that a private purpose was afoot, the hypothetical cases posited by petitioners can be confronted if and when they arise.

[In] affirming the City's authority to take petitioners' properties, we do not minimize the hardship that condemnations may entail, notwithstanding the payment of just compensation. We emphasize that nothing in our opinion precludes any State from placing further restrictions on its exercise of the takings power. [The] necessity and wisdom of using eminent domain to promote economic development are certainly matters of legitimate public debate. This Court's authority, however, extends only to determining whether the City's proposed condemnations are for a "public use" within the meaning of the Fifth Amendment to the Federal Constitution. Because over a century of our case law interpreting that provision dictates an affirmative answer to that question, we may not grant petitioners the relief that they seek.

[Affirmed.]

Justice KENNEDY, concurring.

[A] court applying rational-basis review under the Public Use Clause should strike down a taking that, by a clear showing, is intended to favor a particular private party, with only incidental or pretextual public benefits, just as a court applying rational-basis review under the Equal Protection Clause must strike down a government classification that is clearly intended to injure a particular class of private parties, with only incidental or pretextual public justifications. [A] court confronted with a plausible accusation of impermissible favoritism to private parties should treat the objection as a serious one and review the record to see if it has merit, though with the presumption that the government's actions were reasonable and intended to serve a public purpose. Here, the trial court conducted a careful and extensive inquiry [and concluded] that benefiting Pfizer [or other private entities] was not "the primary motivation or effect of this development plan." [This] case, then, survives the meaningful rational basis review that in my view is required under the Public Use Clause.

[My] agreement with the Court that a presumption of invalidity is not warranted for economic development takings in general, or for the particular takings at issue in this case, does not foreclose the possibility that a more stringent standard of review than that announced in Berman and Midkiff might be appropriate for a more narrowly drawn category of takings. There may be private transfers in which the risk of undetected impermissible favoritism of private parties is so acute that a presumption (rebuttable or otherwise) of invalidity is warranted under the Public Use Clause. This demanding level of scrutiny, however, is not required simply because the purpose of the taking is economic development. [While] there may be categories of cases in which the transfers are so suspicious, or the procedures employed so prone to abuse, or the purported benefits are so trivial or implausible, that courts should presume an impermissible private purpose, no such circumstances are present in this case.

Justice O'CONNOR, with whom Chief Justice REHNQUIST and Justices SCALIA and THOMAS join, dissenting.

[This] case returns us for the first time in over 20 years to the hard question of when a purportedly "public purpose" taking meets the public use requirement. It presents an issue of first impression: Are economic development takings constitutional? I would hold that they are not.

[In Berman and Midkiff], we emphasized the importance of deferring to legislative judgments about public purpose. [Yet] for all the emphasis on deference, Berman and Midkiff hewed to a bedrock principle without which our public use jurisprudence would collapse: "A purely private taking could not withstand the scrutiny of the public use requirement; it would serve no legitimate purpose of government and would thus be void." Midkiff. The Court's holdings in Berman and Midkiff were true to the principle underlying the Public Use Clause. In both those cases, the extraordinary, precondemnation use of the targeted property inflicted affirmative harm on society—in Berman through blight resulting from extreme poverty and in Midkiff through oligopoly resulting from extreme wealth. And in both cases, the relevant legislative body had found that eliminating the existing property use was necessary to remedy the harm. Thus a public purpose was realized when the harmful use was eliminated. Because each taking directly achieved a public benefit, it did not matter that the property was turned over to private use. Here, in contrast, New London does not claim that Susette Kelo's and Wilhelmina Dery's well-maintained homes are the source of any social harm.

[In] moving away from our decisions sanctioning the condemnation of harmful property use, the Court today significantly expands the meaning of public use. It holds that the sovereign may take private property currently put to ordinary private use, and give it over for new, ordinary private use, so long as the new use is predicted to generate some secondary benefit for the public—such as increased tax revenue, more jobs, maybe even aesthetic pleasure. But nearly any lawful use of real private property can be said to generate some incidental benefit to the public. Thus, if predicted (or even guaranteed) positive side-effects are enough to render transfer from one private party to another constitutional, then the words "for public use" do not realistically exclude any takings, and thus do not exert any constraint on the eminent domain power.

[The] logic of today's decision is that eminent domain may only be used to upgrade—not downgrade—property. At best this makes the Public Use Clause redundant with the Due Process Clause, which already prohibits irrational government action. [In] any event, this constraint has no realistic import. For who among us can say she already makes the most productive or attractive possible use of her property? The specter of condemnation hangs over all property. Nothing is to prevent the State from replacing any Motel 6 with a Ritz–Carlton, any home with a shopping mall, or any farm with a factory. Cf. Poletown Neighborhood Council v. Detroit, 410 Mich. 616 (1981) (taking a working-class, immigrant community in Detroit and giving it to a General Motors assembly plant), overruled by County of Wayne v. Hathcock, 471 Mich. 445 (2004).

It was possible after Berman and Midkiff to imagine unconstitutional transfers from A to B. Those decisions endorsed government intervention when private property use had veered to such an extreme that the public was suffering as a consequence. Today nearly all real property is susceptible to condemnation on the Court's theory. In the prescient words of a dissenter from the infamous decision in Poletown, "now that we have authorized local legislative bodies to decide that a different commercial or industrial use of property will produce greater public benefits than its present use, no homeowner's, merchant's or manufacturer's property, however productive or valuable to its owner, is immune from condemnation for the benefit of other private interests that will put it to a 'higher' use." [The] fallout from this decision will not be random. The beneficiaries are likely to be those citizens with disproportionate influence and power in the political process, including large corporations and development firms. As for the victims, the government now has license to transfer property from those with fewer resources to those with more. The Founders cannot have intended this perverse result.

Justice THOMAS, dissenting.

[The] Court replaces the Public Use Clause with a " 'Public Purpose' " Clause [that] enables the Court to hold, against all common sense, that a costly urban-renewal project whose stated purpose is a vague promise of new jobs and increased tax revenue, but which is also suspiciously agreeable to the Pfizer Corporation, is for a "public use." I cannot agree. [Our] cases have strayed from the Clause's original meaning, and I would reconsider them.

[The] Public Use Clause, like the Just Compensation Clause, [is] an express limit on the government's power of eminent domain. The most natural reading of the Clause is that it allows the government to take property only if the government owns, or the public has a legal right to use, the property, as opposed to taking it for any public purpose or necessity whatsoever. [Tellingly,] the phrase "public use" contrasts with the very different phrase "general Welfare" used elsewhere in the Constitution. The Framers would have used some such broader term if they had meant the Public Use Clause to have a similarly sweeping scope. [The Clause is] most naturally read to concern whether the property is used by the public or the government, not whether the purpose of the taking is legitimately public.

[There] is no justification [for] affording almost insurmountable deference to legislative conclusions that a use serves a "public use." [It] is most implausible that the Framers intended to defer to legislatures as to what satisfies the Public Use Clause, uniquely among all the express provisions of the Bill of Rights. We would not defer to a legislature's determination of the various circumstances that establish, for example, when a search of a home would be reasonable. [Yet] today the Court tells us that we are not to "second-guess the City's considered judgments," when the issue is, instead, whether the government may take the infinitely more intrusive step of tearing down petitioners' homes. Something has gone seriously awry with this Court's interpretation of the Constitution.

[More] fundamentally, Berman and Midkiff erred by equating the eminent domain power with the police power of States. See Midkiff ("The 'public use' requirement is . . . coterminous with the scope of a sovereign's police powers"). Traditional uses of that regulatory power, such as the power to abate a nuisance, required no compensation whatsoever, in sharp contrast to the takings power, which has always required compensation. The question whether the State can take property using the power of eminent domain is therefore distinct from the question whether it can regulate property pursuant to the police power. The "public purpose" test applied by Berman and Midkiff also cannot be applied in principled manner. [It] is far easier to analyze whether the government owns or the public has a legal right to use the taken property than to ask whether the taking has a "purely private purpose."

For all these reasons, I would revisit our Public Use Clause cases and consider returning to the original meaning of the Public Use Clause: that the government may take property only if it actually uses or gives the public a legal right to use the property. The consequences of today's decision are not difficult to predict, and promise to be harmful. So-called "urban renewal" programs provide some compensation for the properties they take, but no compensation is possible for the subjective value of these lands to the individuals displaced and the indignity inflicted by uprooting them from their homes. [Extending] the concept of public purpose to encompass any economically beneficial goal guarantees that these losses will fall disproportionately on poor communities. Those communities are not only systematically less likely to put their lands to the highest and best social use, but are also the least politically powerful. If ever there were justification for intrusive judicial review of constitutional provisions that protect "discrete and insular minorities," Carolene Products, surely that principle would apply with great force to the powerless groups and individuals the Public Use Clause protects. [Public] works projects in the 1950's and 1960's destroyed predominantly minority communities in St. Paul, Minnesota, and Baltimore, Maryland. In 1981, urban planners in Detroit, Michigan, uprooted the largely "lower-income and elderly" Poletown neighborhood for the benefit of the General Motors Corporation. Urban renewal projects have long been associated with the displacement of blacks. [Regrettably,] the predictable consequence of the Court's decision will be to exacerbate these effects. [I] would reverse the judgment of the Connecticut Supreme Court.

Page 544. Add after Note 7:

8. *Cabining regulatory takings challenges: rescinding the "substantially advances" test.* In Agins v. City of Tiburon, 447 U.S. 255 (1980), a case involving a takings challenge to zoning ordinances, the Court had stated that "the application of a general zoning law to particular property effects a taking if the ordinance does not substantially advance legitimate state interests, *or* denies an owner economically viable use of his land, see Penn Central" (emphasis added). This disjunctive phrasing had led some lower courts to apply a "substantially advances" test for identifying regulatory takings independent of the factors set forth in Penn Central or the categorical tests set forth in Loretto and Lucas. In LINGLE v. CHEVRON U.S.A. INC., __ U.S. __, 125 S.Ct. 2074 (2005), a unanimous Court made clear that no such separate "substantially advances" test exists. The lower courts in this case had struck down a Hawaii rent control statute as an unconstitutional regulatory taking on the ground that it did not "substantially advance" the State's asserted interest in controlling retail gasoline prices. Justice O'CONNOR wrote for the Court: "Although a number of our takings precedents have recited the 'substantially advances' formula minted in Agins, this is our first opportunity to consider its validity as a freestanding takings test. We conclude that this formula [has] no proper place in our takings jurisprudence. [In] stark contrast to the [regulatory takings tests in Loretto, Lucas and Penn Central,] the 'substantially advances' inquiry reveals nothing about the *magnitude or character of the burden* a particular regulation imposes upon private property rights. Nor does it provide any information about how any regulatory burden is *distributed* among property owners. In consequence, this test does not help to identify those regulations whose effects are functionally comparable to government appropriation or invasion of private property; it is tethered neither to the text of the Takings Clause nor to the basic justification for allowing regulatory actions to be challenged under the Clause.

"[The] 'substantially advances' [test would] also present serious practical difficulties. [It] can be read to demand heightened means-ends review of virtually any regulation of private property. If so interpreted, it would require courts to scrutinize the efficacy of a vast array of state and federal regulations—a task for which courts are not well suited. Moreover, it would empower—and might often require—courts to substitute their predictive judgments for those of elected legislatures and expert agencies. [To] resolve Chevron's takings claim, the District Court was required to choose between the views of two opposing economists as to whether Hawaii's rent control statute would help to prevent concentration and supracompetitive prices in the State's retail gasoline market. Finding one expert to be 'more persuasive' than the other, the court concluded that the Hawaii Legislature's chosen regulatory strategy would not actually achieve its objectives. [We] find the proceedings below remarkable, to say the least, given that we have long eschewed such heightened scrutiny when addressing substantive due process challenges to government regulation. The reasons for deference to legislative judgments about the need for, and likely effectiveness of, regulatory actions are by now well established, and we think they are no less applicable here.''

SECTION 3.   THE REVIVAL OF SUBSTANTIVE DUE PROCESS, FOR NONECONOMIC LIBERTIES: REPRODUCTION; FAMILY; SEX; DEATH

Page 586.   Correct error in listing Justices in partial dissent in Casey:

In place of "Justice WHITE, and Justice THOMAS join, concurring in the judgment in part and dissenting in part," substitute the correct listing as "Justice SCALIA, with whom Chief Justice REHNQUIST, Justice WHITE, and Justice THOMAS join, concurring in the judgment in part and dissenting in part."

SECTION 4.   THE SCOPE OF "LIBERTY" AND "PROPERTY": PROCEDURAL DUE PROCESS AND THE RIGHT TO A HEARING

Page 639.   Add after Note 5:

6. *State law and the scope of "property" interests.* The Roth line of cases established that the Due Process Clause does not protect against deprivation of all government benefits, but only of "entitlements" created by state law. Does a citizen of a state have an enforceable property interest for due process purposes in police enforcement of a restraining order? In TOWN OF CASTLE ROCK v. GONZALES, ___ U.S. ___, 125 S.Ct. 2796 (2005), the Court answered that question negatively, by a vote of 7–2, in a case involving "horrible facts": an estranged husband who, in violation of a restraining order, abducted and killed his three children before being shot and killed by police upon whom he had opened fire. Justice SCALIA wrote for the Court, joined by Chief Justice Rehnquist and Justices O'Connor, Kennedy, Souter, Thomas and Breyer, rejecting a § 1983 claim by the children's mother, Theresa Gonzales: "Respondent claims [that] she had a property interest in police enforcement of the restraining order against her husband; and that the town deprived her of this property without due process by having a policy that tolerated nonenforcement of restraining orders. [Our] cases recognize that a benefit is not a protected entitlement if government officials may grant or deny it in their discretion. [We] do not believe that [Colorado law] made enforcement of restraining orders *mandatory*. A well established tradition of police discretion has long coexisted with apparently mandatory arrest statutes. [Respondent] does not specify the precise means of enforcement that the Colorado restraining-order statute

assertedly mandated—whether her interest lay in having police arrest her husband, having them seek a warrant for his arrest, or having them 'use every reasonable means, up to and including arrest, to enforce the order's terms.' Such indeterminacy is not the hallmark of a duty that is mandatory.

"[Even] if we were to think otherwise concerning the creation of an entitlement by Colorado, it is by no means clear that an individual entitlement to enforcement of a restraining order could constitute a 'property' interest for purposes of the Due Process Clause. Such a right would not, of course, resemble any traditional conception of property. Although that alone does not disqualify it from due process protection, as Roth and its progeny show, the right to have a restraining order enforced does not 'have some ascertainable monetary value,' as even our 'Roth-type property-as-entitlement' cases have implicitly required. Perhaps most radically, the alleged property interest here arises *incidentally,* not out of some new species of government benefit or service, but out of a function that government actors have always performed—to wit, arresting people who they have probable cause to believe have committed a criminal offense. [We] conclude, therefore, that respondent did not, for purposes of the Due Process Clause, have a property interest in police enforcement of the restraining order against her husband."

Justice STEVENS, joined by Justice Ginsburg, dissented, arguing that the issue presented was a narrow one: "It is perfectly clear, on the one hand, that neither the Federal Constitution itself, nor any federal statute, granted respondent or her children any individual entitlement to police protection. Nor, I assume, does any Colorado statute create any such entitlement for the ordinary citizen. On the other hand, it is equally clear that federal law imposes no impediment to the creation of such an entitlement by Colorado law. Respondent certainly could have entered into a contract with a private security firm, obligating the firm to provide protection to respondent's family; respondent's interest in such a contract would unquestionably constitute 'property' within the meaning of the Due Process Clause. If a Colorado statute enacted for her benefit, or a valid order entered by a Colorado judge, created the functional equivalent of such a private contract by granting respondent an entitlement to mandatory individual protection by the local police force, that state-created right would also qualify as 'property' entitled to constitutional protection." The dissenters found such a functional equivalent of a private contract here in light of Colorado's history of tightened procedures for enforcing restraining orders in the context of domestic violence: "Given that Colorado law has quite clearly eliminated the police's discretion to deny enforcement, respondent is correct that she had much more than a 'unilateral expectation' that the restraining order would be enforced; rather, she had a 'legitimate claim of entitlement' to enforcement. Surely, if respondent had contracted with a private security firm to provide her and her daughters with protection from her husband, it would be apparent that she possessed a property interest in such a contract. Here, Colorado undertook a comparable obligation, and respondent—with restraining order in hand—justifiably relied on that undertaking." Justice Souter filed a separate concurrence, joined by Justice Breyer.

CHAPTER 9

EQUAL PROTECTION

SECTION 3. SUSPECT CLASSIFICATIONS: RACE DISCRIMINATION

Page 685. Add to Note 6:

In JOHNSON v. CALIFORNIA, ___ U.S. ___, 125 S.Ct. 1141 (2005), the Court, by a vote of 5–3, held that strict scrutiny must be applied to a state policy of segregating prisoners by race even where preventing racial gang violence was the justification. Justice O'CONNOR wrote for the Court, joined by Justices Kennedy, Souter, Ginsburg, and Breyer: "The California Department of Corrections (CDC) has an unwritten policy of racially segregating prisoners in double cells in reception centers for up to 60 days each time they enter a new correctional facility. [The] CDC's asserted rationale for this practice is that it is necessary to prevent violence caused by racial gangs. [We] have held that 'all racial classifications [imposed by government] . . . must be analyzed by a reviewing court under strict scrutiny.' [The] CDC claims that its policy should be exempt from our categorical rule because it is 'neutral'—that is, [all] prisoners are 'equally' segregated. The CDC's argument ignores our repeated command that 'racial classifications receive close scrutiny even when they may be said to burden or benefit the races equally.' Indeed, we rejected the notion that separate can ever be equal—or 'neutral'—50 years ago in Brown v. Board of Education. [The] need for strict scrutiny is no less important [where] prison officials cite racial violence as the reason for their policy. [Indeed,] by insisting that inmates be housed only with other inmates of the same race, it is possible that prison officials will breed further hostility among prisoners and reinforce racial and ethnic divisions. [When] government officials are permitted to use race as a proxy for gang membership and violence without demonstrating a compelling government interest and proving that their means are narrowly tailored, society as a whole suffers. [In] the prison context, when the government's power is at its apex, we think that searching judicial review of racial classifications is necessary to guard against invidious discrimination. [Strict] scrutiny does not preclude the ability of prison officials to address the compelling interest in prison safety. Prison administrators, however, will have to demonstrate that any race-based policies are narrowly tailored to that end. [Prisons] are dangerous places, and the special circumstances they present may justify racial classifications in some contexts. Such circumstances can be considered in applying strict scrutiny, which is designed to take relevant differences into account." Because the lower courts had reviewed the prison segregation policy under a deferential standard of review derived from challenges to prison regulations in other contexts, the Court remanded for determination of whether California could satisfy strict scrutiny.

Justice STEVENS dissented, insisting that the prison's policy was unconstitutional as an equal protection violation on the record before the Court without need for remand for further fact finding. Justice THOMAS, joined by Justice Scalia, also dissented but in the opposite direction, arguing that strict scrutiny should not apply: "The Constitution has always demanded less within the prison walls. Time and again, even when faced with constitutional rights no less 'fundamental' than the right to be free from state-sponsored racial discrimination, we have deferred to the reasonable judgments of officials experienced in running this Nation's prisons. There is good reason for such deference in this case. California oversees roughly 160,000 inmates, in prisons that have been a breeding ground for some of the most violent prison gangs in America—all of them organized along racial lines. In that atmosphere, California racially segregates a portion of its inmates, in a part of its prisons, for brief periods of up to 60 days, until the State can arrange permanent housing. The majority is concerned with sparing inmates the indignity and stigma of racial discrimination. California is concerned with their safety and saving their lives. I respectfully dissent."

SECTION 5.   THE "FUNDAMENTAL INTERESTS" STRAND OF EQUAL PROTECTION STRICT SCRUTINY

Page 864.   Add after Note 2:

3. *Extending Douglas to some forms of discretionary review.* In HALBERT v. MICHIGAN, ___ U.S. ___, 125 S.Ct. 2582 (2005), the Court revisited the line distinguishing Douglas from Ross. Holding unconstitutional, by a vote of 6–3, Michigan's practice of denying appointed appellate counsel to indigents convicted by guilty or nolo contendere pleas, the Court applied Douglas and distinguished Ross. Justice GINSBURG, joined by Justices Stevens, O'Connor, Kennedy, Souter and Breyer, wrote for the Court: "We hold that Douglas provides the controlling instruction. [A] defendant who pleads guilty or *nolo contendere* in a Michigan court does not thereby forfeit all opportunity for appellate review. Although he relinquishes access to an appeal as of right, he is entitled to apply for leave to appeal, and that entitlement is officially conveyed to him. [Whether] formally categorized as the decision of an appeal or the disposal of a leave application, the Court of Appeals' ruling on a plea-convicted defendant's claims provides the first, and likely the only, direct review the defendant's conviction and sentence will receive. Parties like Halbert, however, are disarmed in their endeavor to gain first-tier review. As the Court in Ross emphasized, a defendant seeking State Supreme Court review following a first-tier appeal as of right earlier had the assistance of appellate counsel [and] may also be armed with an opinion of the intermediate appellate court addressing the issues counsel raised. A first-tier review applicant, forced to act *pro se*, will face a record unreviewed by appellate counsel, and will be equipped with no attorney's brief prepared for, or reasoned opinion by, a court of review. Persons in Halbert's situation are particularly handicapped as self-representatives. [Navigating] the appellate process without a lawyer's assistance is a perilous endeavor for a layperson, and well beyond the competence of individuals, like Halbert, who have little education, learning disabilities, and mental impair-

ments.'' She concluded that the Due Process and Equal Protection Clauses require the appointment of counsel for defendants seeking first-tier review from convictions on pleas.

Justice THOMAS, joined by Chief Justice Rehnquist and Scalia, dissented: ''Douglas [does] not support extending the right to counsel to any form of discretionary review, as Ross v. Moffitt, and later cases make clear. Moreover, Michigan has not engaged in the sort of invidious discrimination against indigent defendants that Douglas condemns. Michigan has done no more than recognize the undeniable difference between defendants who plead guilty and those who maintain their innocence, in an attempt to divert resources from largely frivolous appeals to more meritorious ones. The majority substitutes its own policy preference for that of Michigan voters, and it does so based on an untenable reading of Douglas. [Admittedly,] the precise rationale for the Griffin/Douglas line of cases has never been made explicit. Those cases, however, have a common theme. States may not impose financial barriers that preclude indigent defendants from securing appellate review altogether. Nor may States create 'unreasoned distinctions' among defendants that 'arbitrarily cut off appeal rights for indigents while leaving open avenues of appeals for more affluent persons.' Far from being an 'arbitrary' or 'unreasoned' distinction, Michigan's differentiation between defendants convicted at trial and defendants convicted by plea is sensible. [Lacking] support in this Court's cases, the majority effects a not-so-subtle shift from whether the record is adequate to enable discretionary review to whether plea-convicted defendants are generally able to 'naviga[te] the appellate process without a lawyer's assistance.' This rationale lacks any stopping point. *Pro se* defendants may have difficulty navigating discretionary direct appeals and collateral proceedings, but this Court has never extended the right to counsel beyond first appeals as of right.''

FREEDOM OF SPEECH—HOW GOVERNMENT RESTRICTS SPEECH—MODES OF ABRIDGMENT AND STANDARDS OF REVIEW

SECTION 2. GOVERNMENT'S POWER TO LIMIT SPEECH IN ITS CAPACITY AS PROPRIETOR, EDUCATOR, EMPLOYER AND PATRON

Page 1312. Add after US v. NTEU:

In contrast to the broad approach taken in NTEU, the Court made clear in CITY OF SAN DIEGO v. ROE, ___ U.S. ___, 125 S.Ct. 521 (2004) (per curiam), that there are limits to the scope of matters of public concern on which public employees may make commentary in their capacity as citizens. The case involved a San Diego police officer who made videos of himself stripping off a police uniform and masturbating, including while issuing a traffic ticket, and sold them online on eBay, listing himself in his user profile as in the field of law enforcement. He was terminated from the police force, and alleged that the termination violated his right to free speech. The Court reversed a Ninth Circuit opinion that had deemed his off-duty, off-premises speech protected under Pickering and NTEU: "The Court of Appeals' reliance on NTEU was seriously misplaced. Although Roe's activities took place outside the workplace and purported to be about subjects not related to his employment, the SDPD demonstrated legitimate and substantial interests of its own that were compromised by his speech. Far from confining his activities to speech unrelated to his employment, Roe took deliberate steps to link his videos [to] his police work, all in a way injurious to his employer. [The] present case falls outside the protection afforded in NTEU." The Court went on to clarify that not all public employee speech that is unrelated to internal workplace grievances under Connick is automatically entitled to Pickering review: "Pickering did not hold that any and all statements by a public employee are entitled to balancing. [In] order to merit Pickering balancing, a public employee's speech must touch on a matter of 'public concern.' [P]ublic concern is something that is a subject of legitimate news interest, that is, a subject of general interest and of value and concern to the public at the time of publication. [Applying] these principles to the instant case, there is no difficulty in concluding that Roe's expression does not qualify as a matter of public concern under any view of the public concern test. He fails the threshold test and Pickering balancing does not come into play."

CHAPTER 13

Rights Ancillary to Freedom of Speech

Section 2.   Freedom of Association

Page 1415.   Add to end of Note 2:

A third free speech challenge to advertising exactions under federal agricultural marketing orders, this time to those used for beef promotion including the slogan "Beef—It's What's for Dinner," made its way to the Court in JOHANNS v. LIVESTOCK MARKETING ASSOCIATION, ___ U.S. ___, 125 S.Ct. 2055 (2005). This time the decision, like that in Glickman and unlike that in United Foods, came down in favor of the government. But the Court expressly disclaimed reliance on Glickman, noting that, while Glickman had found that "compelled support for generic advertising was legitimately part of the Government's 'collectivist' centralization of the market for tree fruit," here, as in United Foods, "there is no broader regulatory system in place that collectivizes aspects of the beef market unrelated to speech, so Glickman is not controlling." Instead, the Court rested its rejection of the free speech challenge on the notion that the beef exaction, like taxation, supported *government* speech. Justice SCALIA wrote the opinion of the Court, which was joined by Chief Justice Rehnquist and Justices O'Connor, Thomas and Breyer: "In all of the cases invalidating exactions to subsidize speech, the speech was, or was presumed to be, that of an entity other than the government itself. Keller, Abood, United Foods, Southworth. Our compelled-subsidy cases have consistently respected the principle that 'compelled support of a private association is fundamentally different from compelled support of government.' 'Compelled support of government'—even those programs of government one does not approve—is of course perfectly constitutional, as every taxpayer must attest. [We] have generally assumed, though not yet squarely held, that compelled funding of government speech does not alone raise First Amendment concerns."

Applying these principles, Justice Scalia concluded that the beef exactions supported the speech of the government, not of the Beef Board, a nongovernmental entity that was delegated some responsibility over the advertising: "The message of the promotional campaigns is effectively controlled by the Federal Government itself. The message set out in the beef promotions is from beginning to end the message established by the Federal Government. [Congress] and the Secretary have set out the overarching message [and] the Secretary exercises final approval authority over every word used in every promotional campaign." Justice Scalia also rejected the cattle growers' contention "that the beef program does not qualify as 'government speech' because it is funded by a targeted assessment on beef producers, rather than by general revenues'': ''The compelled-*subsidy* analysis is altogether unaffected by whether the funds for the promotions are raised by general taxes or through a targeted assessment. [The] First Amendment does not confer a right to pay one's taxes into the general fund, because the injury of compelled funding [does] not stem from the Government's mode of accounting. [Here,] the beef advertisements are subject to political safeguards more than adequate to set them apart from private messages.'' The majority declined to reach the cattle growers' additional argument that ''crediting the advertising to 'America's Beef Producers' impermissibly uses not only their money but also their seeming endorsement to promote a message with which they do not agree,'' reasoning that this compelled-speech as opposed to compelled-subsidy argument was not appropriate on a facial challenge, ''[s]ince neither the Beef Act nor the Beef Order *requires* attribution.'' The opinion noted that such an argument might form the basis for an as-applied challenge if it were established that individual advertisements were attributed to the challengers.

Justice THOMAS concurred, reiterating that he would hold compelled advertising exactions subject to strict First Amendment scrutiny but recognized ''that this principle must be qualified where the regulation compels the funding of speech that is the government's own.'' Justice BREYER filed a concurrence stating that the beef program was analytically indistinguishable from the mushroom program struck down in United Foods, and reiterated his position in dissent from United Foods that the challenged assessments in both cases ''involved a form of economic regulation, not speech.'' Justice GINSBURG concurred only in the judgment: ''I resist ranking the promotional messages funded under the [Beef Act], but not attributed to the Government, as government speech, given the message the Government conveys in its own name [urging the American public to limit intake of fatty foods]. I remain persuaded, however, that the assessments in these cases, as in [United Foods and Glickman] qualify as permissible economic regulation.''

Justice SOUTER dissented, joined by Justices Stevens and Kennedy: ''The ranchers' complaint is on all fours with the objection of the mushroom growers in United Foods, where a similar statutory exaction was struck down as a compelled subsidy of speech prohibited by the First Amendment absent a comprehensive regulatory scheme to which the speech was incidental. [The] Court accepts the [government-speech] defense unwisely. [I] take the view that if government relies on the government-speech doctrine to compel specific groups to fund speech with targeted taxes, it must make itself politically accountable by indicating that the content actually is a government message, not just the statement of one self-interested group the government is currently willing to invest with power. [Because] the Beef Act fails to require the Government to show its hand, I would [hold] the Act unconstitutional. [The] ads are not required to show any sign of being speech by the Government, and [the] tag line, 'funded by America's Beef Producers,' [all] but ensures that no one reading them will suspect that the message comes from the National Government [rather than] the beef producers who stand to profit when beef is on the table. No one hearing a commercial for Pepsi or Levi's thinks Uncle Sam is the man talking behind the curtain. Why would a person reading a beef ad think Uncle Sam was trying to make him eat more steak? [It] means nothing that Government officials control the message if that fact is never required to be made apparent to those who get the message, let alone if it is affirmatively concealed from them.'' Justice Kennedy also filed a brief dissent.

Page 1424.   Add at end of Note 4:

In the Court's most recent decision concerning political party primaries, the Court ruled, by a vote of 6–3, that Oklahoma's semiclosed primary law did not violate the freedom of political association. The system provided that a political party may invite only its own party members and voters registered as Independents to vote in the party's primary. Under that system, the Libertarian Party of Oklahoma (LPO) was prevented from inviting Republicans and Democrats as well as registered Independents from voting in its primary elections. Writing for the Court in CLINGMAN v. BEAVER, ___ U.S. ___, 125 S.Ct. 2029 (2005), Justice THOMAS upheld this barrier, writing for the Court in an opinion joined by Chief Justice Rehnquist and Justices Scalia, and Kennedy, and in relevant part by Justices O'Connor and Breyer. He distinguished Tashjian as involving more severe burdens on political association: ''Connecticut's closed primary limited citizens' freedom of political association [by requiring] Independent voters to affiliate publicly with a party to vote in its primary. That is not true in this case. At issue here are voters who have *already* affiliated publicly with one of Oklahoma's political parties. [These] minor barriers between voter and party do not compel strict scrutiny.'' Applying a more deferential standard of review, Justice Thomas found reasonable and politically neutral Oklahoma's regulatory interests in preserving the identity of political parties and aiding their efforts at electioneering and party-building.

Justice STEVENS dissented, joined by Justices Souter and Ginsburg: ''The Court's decision today diminishes the value of two important rights protected by the First Amendment: the individual citizen's right to vote for the candidate of her choice and a political party's right to define its own mission. No one would contend that a citizen's membership in either the Republican or the Democratic Party could disqualify her from attending political functions sponsored by another party, or from voting for a third party's candidate in a general election. If a third party invites her to participate in its primary election, her right to support the candidate of her choice merits constitutional protection, whether she elects to make a speech, to donate funds, or to cast a ballot. The importance of vindicating that individual right far outweighs any public interest in punishing registered Republicans or Democrats for acts of disloyalty. [This] is not to say that voters have an absolute right to participate in whatever primary they desire. For instance, the parties themselves have a strong associational interest in determining which individuals may vote in their primaries, and that interest will normally outweigh the interest of the uninvited voter. But in the ordinary case the State simply has no interest in classifying voters by their political party and in limiting the elections in which voters may participate as a result of that classification. [In] addition to burdening the individual respondent's right to vote, the Oklahoma scheme places a heavy burden on the LPO's associational rights.'' He would have found the associational interests at stake ''virtually identical'' to those in Tashjian, and found the state interests so ''speculative or simply protectionist'' of the parties in power that, ''[n]o matter what the standard, they simply do not outweigh the interests of the LPO and its voters.''

CHAPTER 14

THE RELIGION CLAUSES: FREE EXERCISE AND ESTABLISHMENT

SECTION 3. THE ESTABLISHMENT CLAUSE

Page 1580. Add after Capitol Square Review Bd. v. Pinette:

McCreary County v. ACLU of Kentucky

___ U.S. ___, 125 S.Ct. 2722 (2005).

Justice SOUTER delivered the opinion of the court [in which Justices STEVENS, O'CONNOR, GINSBURG, and BREYER joined.]

Executives of two counties posted a version of the Ten Commandments on the walls of their courthouses. After suits were filed charging violations of the Establishment Clause, the legislative body of each county adopted a resolution calling for a more extensive exhibit meant to show that the Commandments are Kentucky's "precedent legal code." The result in each instance was a modified display of the Commandments surrounded by texts containing religious references as their sole common element. After changing counsel, the counties revised the exhibits again by eliminating some documents, expanding the text set out in another, and adding some new ones.

The issues are whether a determination of the counties' purpose is a sound basis for ruling on the Establishment Clause complaints, and whether evaluation of the counties' claim of secular purpose for the ultimate displays may take their evolution into account. We hold that the counties' manifest objective may be dispositive of the constitutional enquiry, and that the development of the presentation should be considered when determining its purpose.

I. In the summer of 1999, petitioners McCreary County and Pulaski County, Kentucky (hereinafter Counties), put up in their respective courthouses large, gold-framed copies of an abridged text of the King James version of the Ten Commandments, including a citation to the Book of Exodus. [In] each county, the hallway display was "readily visible to . . . county citizens who use the courthouse to conduct their civic business." [In] November 1999, respondents American Civil Liberties Union of Kentucky sued the Counties in Federal District Court. Within a month, [the] legislative body of each County authorized a second, expanded display, by nearly identical resolutions reciting that the Ten Commandments are "the precedent legal code upon which the civil and criminal codes of . . . Kentucky are founded." [As] directed by the resolutions, the Counties expanded the displays of the Ten Commandments in their locations, presumably along with copies of the resolution, which instructed that it, too, be posted. After [the] District Court [ordered] that the "display

... be removed from [each] County Courthouse," [the] Counties [installed] another display in each courthouse, [consisting] of nine framed documents of equal size, one of them setting out the Ten Commandments explicitly identified as the "King James Version" at Exodus 20:3–17. Assembled with the Commandments are framed copies of the Magna Carta, the Declaration of Independence, the Bill of Rights, the lyrics of the Star Spangled Banner, the Mayflower Compact, the National Motto, the Preamble to the Kentucky Constitution, and a picture of Lady Justice.

II. [The] touchstone for our analysis is the principle that the "First Amendment mandates governmental neutrality between religion and religion, and between religion and nonreligion." When the government acts with the ostensible and predominant purpose of advancing religion, it violates that central Establishment Clause value of official religious neutrality, there being no neutrality when the government's ostensible object is to take sides. [By] showing a purpose to favor religion, the government "sends the . . . message to . . . nonadherents 'that they are outsiders, not full members of the political community, and an accompanying message to adherents that they are insiders, favored members. . . .' "

[Despite] the intuitive importance of official purpose to the realization of Establishment Clause values, the Counties ask us to abandon Lemon's purpose test, or at least to truncate any enquiry into purpose here. [They argue] true "purpose" is unknowable, and its search merely an excuse for courts to act selectively and unpredictably in picking out evidence of subjective intent. The assertions are as seismic as they are unconvincing. Examination of purpose is a staple of statutory interpretation that makes up the daily fare of every appellate court in the country, and governmental purpose is a key element of a good deal of constitutional doctrine. [In] Establishment Clause analysis [an] understanding of official objective emerges from readily discoverable fact, without any judicial psychoanalysis of a drafter's heart of hearts. The eyes that look to purpose belong to an " 'objective observer,' " one who takes account of the traditional external signs that show up in the " 'text, legislative history, and implementation of the statute,' " or comparable official act. [Nor] is there any indication that the enquiry is rigged in practice to finding a religious purpose dominant every time a case is filed. In the past, the test has not been fatal very often, presumably because government does not generally act unconstitutionally, with the predominant purpose of advancing religion.

After declining the invitation to abandon concern with purpose wholesale, we also have to avoid the Counties' alternative tack of trivializing the enquiry into it. The Counties would read the cases as if the purpose enquiry were so naive that any transparent claim to secularity would satisfy it, and they would cut context out of the enquiry, to the point of ignoring history, no matter what bearing it actually had on the significance of current circumstances. [The] world is not made brand new every morning, and the Counties [want] an absentminded objective observer, not one presumed to be familiar with the history of the government's actions and competent to learn what history has to show. The Counties' position just bucks common sense: reasonable observers have reasonable memories, and our precedents sensibly forbid an observer "to turn a blind eye to the context in which [the] policy arose."

III. We take Stone [v. Graham (1980); 15th ed., p. 1561], as the initial legal benchmark, our only case dealing with the constitutionality of displaying the Commandments. Stone recognized that the Commandments are an "instrument of religion." [But] Stone did not purport to decide the constitutionality of every possible way the Commandments might be set out by the government, and under the Establishment Clause detail is key. Hence, we look to the record of evidence showing the progression leading up to the third display of the Commandments.

The display rejected in Stone had two obvious similarities to the first one in the sequence here: both set out a text of the Commandments as distinct from any traditionally symbolic representation, and each stood alone, not part of an arguably secular display. Stone stressed the significance of integrating the Commandments into a secular scheme to forestall the broadcast of an otherwise clearly religious message and for good reason, the Commandments being a central point of reference in the religious and moral history of Jews and Christians. They proclaim the existence of a monotheistic god (no other gods). They regulate details of religious obligation (no graven images, no sabbath breaking, no vain oath swearing). And they unmistakably rest even the universally accepted prohibitions (as against murder, theft, and the like) on the sanction of the divinity proclaimed at the beginning of the text. [The] Counties' solo exhibit here did nothing more to counter the sectarian implication than the postings at issue in Stone. [When] the government initiates an effort to place this statement alone in public view, a religious object is unmistakable.

[In the] second display, unlike the first, the Commandments were not hung in isolation, [but] include[d] the statement of the government's purpose expressly set out in the county resolutions, and underscored it by juxtaposing the Commandments to other documents with highlighted references to God as their sole common element. The display's unstinting focus was on religious passages, showing that the Counties were posting the Commandments precisely because of their sectarian content. That demonstration of the government's objective was enhanced by serial religious references and the accompanying resolution's claim about the embodiment of ethics in Christ. Together, the display and resolution presented an indisputable, and undisputed, showing of an impermissible purpose.

[After] the Counties changed lawyers, they mounted a third display, without a new resolution or repeal of the old one. The result was the "Foundations of American Law and Government" exhibit, which placed the Commandments in the company of other documents the Counties thought especially significant in the historical foundation of American government. [The] extraordinary resolutions for the second display passed just months earlier were not repealed or otherwise repudiated. Indeed, the sectarian spirit of the common resolution found enhanced expression in the third display, which quoted more of the purely religious language of the Commandments than the first two displays had done. No reasonable observer could swallow the claim that the Counties had cast off the objective so unmistakable in the earlier displays. [He] would probably suspect that the Counties were simply reaching for any way to keep a religious document on the walls of courthouses constitutionally required to embody religious neutrality.

[We] do not decide that the Counties' past actions forever taint any effort on their part to deal with the subject matter. We hold only that purpose needs to be taken seriously under the Establishment Clause and needs to be understood in light of context; an implausible claim that governmental purpose has changed should not carry the day in a court of law any more than in a head with common sense. [Nor] do we have occasion here to hold that a sacred text can never be integrated constitutionally into a governmental display on the subject of law, or American history. We do not forget, and in this litigation have frequently been reminded, that our own courtroom frieze was deliberately designed in the exercise of governmental authority so as to include the figure of Moses holding tablets exhibiting a portion of the Hebrew text of the later, secularly phrased Commandments; in the company of 17 other lawgivers, most of them secular figures, there is no risk that Moses would strike an observer as evidence that the National Government was violating neutrality in religion.

IV. [The dissent] puts forward a limitation on the application of the neutrality principle, with citations to historical evidence said to show that the Framers understood the ban on establishment of religion as sufficiently narrow to allow the government to espouse submission to the divine will. [But] the dissent's argument for the original understanding is flawed from the outset by its failure to consider the full range of evidence showing what the Framers believed. [There] is also evidence supporting the proposition that the Framers intended the Establishment Clause to require governmental neutrality in matters of religion, including neutrality in statements acknowledging religion. [Jefferson] refused to issue Thanksgiving Proclamations because he believed that they violated the Constitution. And Madison [criticized] Virginia's general assessment tax not just because it required people to donate "three pence" to religion, but because "it is itself a signal of persecution. It degrades from the equal rank of Citizens all those whose opinions in Religion do not bend to those of the Legislative authority." The fair inference is that there was no common understanding about the limits of the establishment prohibition, and the dissent's conclusion that its narrower view was the original understanding stretches the evidence beyond tensile capacity.

[While] the dissent fails to show a consistent original understanding from which to argue that the neutrality principle should be rejected, it does manage to deliver a surprise [in saying] that the deity the Framers had in mind was the God of monotheism, with the consequence that government may espouse a tenet of traditional monotheism. This is truly a remarkable view. [It] apparently means that government should be free to approve the core beliefs of a favored religion over the tenets of others, a view that should trouble anyone who prizes religious liberty. Certainly history cannot justify it; on the contrary, history shows that the religion of concern to the Framers was not that of the monotheistic faiths generally, but Christianity in particular, a fact that no member of this Court takes as a premise for construing the Religion Clauses.

[We] are centuries away from the St. Bartholomew's Day massacre and the treatment of heretics in early Massachusetts, but the divisiveness of religion in current public life is inescapable. This is no time to deny the prudence of understanding the Establishment Clause to require the Government to stay neutral on religious belief, which is reserved for the conscience of the individual.

[Affirmed.]

Justice O'CONNOR, concurring.

[Reasonable] minds can disagree about how to apply the Religion Clauses in a given case. But the goal of the Clauses is clear: to carry out the Founders' plan of preserving religious liberty to the fullest extent possible in a pluralistic society. By enforcing the Clauses, we have kept religion a matter for the individual conscience, not for the prosecutor or bureaucrat. At a time when we see around the world the violent consequences of the assumption of religious authority by government, Americans may count themselves fortunate: Our regard for constitutional boundaries has protected us from similar travails, while allowing private religious exercise to flourish. [Those] who would renegotiate the boundaries between church and state must therefore answer a difficult question: Why would we trade a system that has served us so well for one that has served others so poorly?

[Given] the history of this particular display of the Ten Commandments, the Court correctly finds an Establishment Clause violation. The purpose behind the counties' display is relevant because it conveys an unmistakable message of endorsement to the reasonable observer. It is true that many Americans find the Commandments in accord with their personal beliefs. But we do not count heads before enforcing the First Amendment. Nor can we accept the theory that Americans who do not accept the Commandments' validity are outside the First Amendment's protections. [It] is true that the Framers lived at a time when our national religious diversity was neither as robust nor as well recognized as it is now. They may not have foreseen the variety of religions for which this Nation would eventually provide a home. They surely could not have predicted new religions, some of them born in this country. But they did know that line-drawing between religions is an enterprise that, once begun, has no logical stopping point. [The] Religion Clauses, as a result, protect adherents of all religions, as well as those who believe in no religion at all.

Justice SCALIA, with whom Chief Justice REHNQUIST and Justice THOMAS join, and with whom Justice KENNEDY joins as to Parts II and III, dissenting.

I.   On September 11, 2001 I was attending in Rome, Italy an international conference of judges and lawyers, principally from Europe and the United States. That night and the next morning virtually all of the participants watched, in their hotel rooms, the address to the Nation by the President of the United States concerning the murderous attacks upon the Twin Towers and the Pentagon, in which thousands of Americans had been killed. The address ended, as Presidential addresses often do, with the prayer "God bless America." The next afternoon I was approached by one of the judges from a European country, who, after extending his profound condolences for my country's loss, sadly observed "How I wish that the Head of State of my country, at a similar time of national tragedy and distress, could conclude his address 'God bless _____.' It is of course absolutely forbidden." That is one model of the relationship between church and state—a model spread across Europe by the armies of Napoleon, and reflected in the Constitution of France, which begins "France is [a] ... secular ... Republic." Religion is to be strictly excluded from the public forum. This is not, and never was, the model adopted by America. George Washington added to the [Presidential oath] the concluding words "so help me God." The Supreme Court under John Marshall opened its sessions with the prayer, "God save the United States and this Honorable Court." The First Congress instituted the practice of beginning its legislative sessions with a prayer. [The] day after the First Amendment was proposed, the same Congress that had proposed it requested the President to proclaim "a day of public thanksgiving and prayer, to be observed, by acknowledging, with grateful hearts, the many and signal favours of Almighty God." [And] of course the First Amendment itself accords religion (and no other manner of belief) special constitutional protection.

These actions of our First President and Congress and the Marshall Court were not idiosyncratic; they reflected the beliefs of the period. Those who wrote the Constitution believed that morality was essential to the well-being of society and that encouragement of religion was the best way to foster morality. [Nor] have the views of our people on this matter significantly changed. Presidents continue to conclude the Presidential oath with the words "so help me God." Our legislatures, state and national, continue to open their sessions with prayer led by official chaplains. The sessions of this Court continue to open with the prayer "God save the United States and this Honorable Court." Invocation of the Almighty by our public figures, at all levels of government, remains commonplace. Our coinage bears the motto "IN GOD WE TRUST." And our Pledge of Allegiance contains the acknowledgment that we are a Nation "under God." With all of this reality (and much more) staring it in the face, how can the Court possibly assert that " 'the First Amendment mandates governmental neutrality between … religion and nonreligion,' " and that "manifesting a purpose to favor … adherence to religion generally," is unconstitutional?

[Besides] appealing to the demonstrably false principle that the government cannot favor religion over irreligion, today's opinion suggests that the posting of the Ten Commandments violates the principle that the government cannot favor one religion over another. That is indeed a valid principle where public aid or assistance to religion is concerned, see Zelman v. Simmons–Harris (2002) [15th ed., p. 1599], or where the free exercise of religion is at issue, Church of Lukumi Babalu Aye, Inc. v. Hialeah (1993) [15th ed.; p. 1514], but it necessarily applies in a more limited sense to public acknowledgment of the Creator. If religion in the public forum had to be entirely nondenominational, there could be no religion in the public forum at all. One cannot say the word "God," or "the Almighty," without contradicting the beliefs of some people that there are many gods, or that God or the gods pay no attention to human affairs. Historical practices [demonstrate] that there is a distance between the acknowledgment of a single Creator and the establishment of a religion. [The] three most popular religions in the United States, Christianity, Judaism, and Islam—which combined account for 97.7% of all believers—are monotheistic. All of them, moreover (Islam included), believe that the Ten Commandments were given by God to Moses, and are divine prescriptions for a virtuous life. Publicly honoring the Ten Commandments is thus indistinguishable, insofar as discriminating against other religions is concerned, from publicly honoring God. Both practices are recognized across such a broad and diverse range of the population—from Christians to Muslims—that they cannot be reasonably understood as a government endorsement of a particular religious viewpoint.[1]

[Justice Stevens asserts] that I would "marginalize the belief systems of more than 7 million Americans" who adhere to religions that are not monotheistic. Surely that is a gross exaggeration. The beliefs of those citizens are entirely protected by the Free Exercise Clause, and by those aspects of the Establishment Clause that do not relate to government acknowledgment of the Creator. [Justice Stevens] fails to recognize that in the context of public acknowledgments of God there are legitimate competing interests: On the one hand, the interest of that minority in not feeling "excluded"; but on the other, the interest of the overwhelming majority of religious believers in being able to give God thanks and supplication as a people, and with respect to our national endeavors. Our national tradition has resolved that conflict in favor of the majority.

II. [As] bad as the Lemon test is, it is worse for the fact that, since its inception, its seemingly simple mandates have been manipulated to fit whatever result the Court aimed to achieve. Today's opinion is no different. In two respects it modifies Lemon to ratchet up the Court's hostility to religion. First, the Court justifies inquiry into legislative purpose, not as an end itself, but as a means to ascertain the appearance of the government action to an " 'objective observer.' " [Under] this approach, even if a government could show that its actual purpose was not to advance religion, it would presumably violate the Constitution as long as the Court's objective observer would think otherwise. [Second,] the Court replaces Lemon's requirement that the government have "a secular . . . purpose," with the heightened requirement that the secular purpose "predominate" over any purpose to advance religion. [The] new demand that secular purpose predominate contradicts Lemon's more limited requirement, and finds no support in our cases. In all but one of the five cases in which this Court has invalidated a government practice on the basis of its purpose to benefit religion, it has first declared that the statute was motivated entirely by the desire to advance religion. See Santa Fe, Wallace, Stone, Epperson. [I] have urged that Lemon's purpose prong be abandoned, because [even] an exclusive purpose to foster or assist religious practice is not necessarily invalidating. But today's extension makes things even worse. [Those] responsible for the adoption of the Religion Clauses would surely regard it as a bitter irony that the religious values they designed those Clauses to protect have now become so distasteful to this Court that if they constitute anything more than a subordinate motive for government action they will invalidate it.

III. Even accepting the Court's Lemon-based premises, the displays at issue here were constitutional. To any person who happened to walk down the hallway of the McCreary or Pulaski County Courthouse during the roughly nine months when the Foundations Displays were exhibited, the displays must

---

1. This is not to say that a display of the Ten Commandments could never constitute an impermissible endorsement of a particular religious view. The Establishment Clause would prohibit, for example, governmental endorsement of a particular version of the Decalogue as authoritative. Here the display of the Ten Commandments alongside eight secular documents, and the plaque's explanation for their inclusion, make clear that they were not posted to take sides in a theological dispute. [Footnote by Justice Scalia.]

have seemed unremarkable—if indeed they were noticed at all. The walls of both courthouses were already lined with historical documents and other assorted portraits; each Foundations Display was exhibited in the same format as these other displays and nothing in the record suggests that either County took steps to give it greater prominence.

[On] its face, the Foundations Displays manifested the purely secular purpose that the Counties asserted before the District Court: "to display documents that played a significant role in the foundation of our system of law and government." That the Displays included the Ten Commandments did not transform their apparent secular purpose into one of impermissible advocacy for Judeo–Christian beliefs. [When] the Ten Commandments appear alongside other documents of secular significance in a display devoted to the foundations of American law and government, the context communicates that the Ten Commandments are included, not to teach their binding nature as a religious text, but to show their unique contribution to the development of the legal system. [The] acknowledgment of the contribution that religion in general, and the Ten Commandments in particular, have made to our Nation's legal and governmental heritage is surely no more of a step towards establishment of religion than was the practice of legislative prayer we approved in Marsh v. Chambers, and it seems to be on par with the inclusion of a creche or a menorah in a "Holiday" display that incorporates other secular symbols, see Lynch, Allegheny County.

[In] any event, the Court's conclusion that the Counties exhibited the Foundations Displays with the purpose of promoting religion is doubtful. [If] the Commandments have a proper place in our civic history, even placing them by themselves can be civically motivated—especially when they are placed, not in a school (as they were in the Stone case upon which the Court places such reliance), but in a courthouse. [The] first displays did not necessarily evidence an intent to further religious practice; nor did the second displays, or the resolutions authorizing them; and there is in any event no basis for attributing whatever intent motivated the first and second displays to the third.

Van Orden v. Perry

__ U.S. __, 125 S.Ct. 2854 (2005).

Chief Justice REHNQUIST announced the judgment of the court and delivered an opinion, in which Justices SCALIA, KENNEDY, and THOMAS join.

The question here is whether the Establishment Clause of the First Amendment allows the display of a monument inscribed with the Ten Commandments on the Texas State Capitol grounds. We hold that it does.

The 22 acres surrounding the Texas State Capitol contain 17 monuments and 21 historical markers commemorating the "people, ideals, and events that compose Texan identity." The monolith challenged here stands 6–feet high and 3–feet wide. It is located to the north of the Capitol building, between the Capitol and the Supreme Court building. Its primary content is the text of the Ten Commandments.

[This case presents] us with the difficulty of respecting both faces [of the Establishment Clause]. Our institutions presuppose a Supreme Being, yet these institutions must not press religious observances upon their citizens. One face looks to the past in acknowledgment of our Nation's heritage, while the other looks to the present in demanding a separation between church and state. Reconciling these two faces requires that we neither abdicate our responsibility to maintain a division between church and state nor evince a hostility to religion by disabling the government from in some ways recognizing our religious heritage.

[Whatever] may be the fate of the Lemon test in the larger scheme of Establishment Clause jurisprudence, we think it not useful in dealing with the sort of passive monument that Texas has erected on its Capitol grounds. Instead, our analysis is driven both by the nature of the monument and by our Nation's history. As we explained in Lynch v. Donnelly: "There is an unbroken history of official acknowledgment by all three branches of government of the role of religion in American life from at least 1789." [Recognition] of the role of God in our Nation's heritage has also been reflected in our decisions. [Marsh ; McGowan.]

In this case we are faced with a display of the Ten Commandments on government property outside the Texas State Capitol. Such acknowledgments of the role played by the Ten Commandments in our Nation's heritage are common throughout America. We need only look within our own Courtroom. Since 1935, Moses has stood, holding two tablets that reveal portions of the Ten Commandments written in Hebrew, among other lawgivers in the south frieze. Representations of the Ten Commandments adorn the metal gates lining the north and south sides of the Courtroom as well as the doors leading into the Courtroom. Moses also sits on the exterior east facade of the building holding the Ten Commandments tablets.

[Of course,] the Ten Commandments are religious—they were so viewed at their inception and so remain. The monument, therefore, has religious significance. According to Judeo–Christian belief, the Ten Commandments were given to Moses by God on Mt. Sinai. But Moses was a lawgiver as well as a religious leader. And the Ten Commandments have an undeniable historical meaning, as the foregoing examples demonstrate. Simply having religious content or promoting a message consistent with a religious doctrine does not run afoul of the Establishment Clause.

There are, of course, limits to the display of religious messages or symbols. For example, we held unconstitutional a Kentucky statute requiring the posting of the Ten Commandments in every public schoolroom. Stone v. Graham. [Neither] Stone itself nor subsequent opinions have indicated that Stone's holding would extend to a legislative chamber. The placement of the Ten Commandments monument on the Texas State Capitol grounds is a far more passive use of those texts than was the case in Stone, where the text confronted elementary school students every day. The monument is therefore also quite different from the prayers involved in Schempp and Lee v. Weisman. Texas has treated her Capitol grounds monuments as representing the several strands in the State's political and legal history. The inclusion of the Ten Commandments monument in this group has a dual significance, partaking of both religion and government. We cannot say that Texas' display of this monument violates the Establishment Clause of the First Amendment.

[Affirmed.]

Justice SCALIA, concurring.

I join the opinion of the Chief Justice because I think it accurately reflects our current Establishment Clause jurisprudence—or at least the Establishment Clause jurisprudence we currently apply some of the time. I would prefer to reach the same result by adopting an Establishment Clause jurisprudence that is in accord with our Nation's past and present practices, and that can be consistently applied—the central relevant feature of which is that there is nothing unconstitutional in a State's favoring religion generally, honoring God through public prayer and acknowledgment, or, in a nonproselytizing manner, venerating the Ten Commandments.

Justice THOMAS, concurring.

[This] case would be easy if the Court were willing to abandon the inconsistent guideposts it has adopted for addressing Establishment Clause challenges, and return to the original meaning of the Clause. I have previously suggested that the Clause's text and history "resist incorporation" against the States. If the Establishment Clause does not restrain the States, then it has no application here, where only state action is at issue.

Even if the Clause is incorporated, or if the Free Exercise Clause limits the power of States to establish religions, our task would be far simpler if we returned to the original meaning of the word "establishment" than it is under the various approaches this Court now uses. The Framers understood an establishment "necessarily [to] involve actual legal coercion." There is no question that, based on the original meaning of the Establishment Clause, the Ten Commandments display at issue here is constitutional. In no sense does Texas compel petitioner Van Orden to do anything. The only injury to him is that he takes offense at seeing the monument as he passes it on his way to the Texas Supreme Court Library. He need not stop to read it or even to look at it, let alone to express support for it or adopt the Commandments as guides for his life. The mere presence of the monument along his path involves no coercion and thus does not violate the Establishment Clause.

Justice BREYER, concurring in the judgment.

[If] the relation between government and religion is one of separation, but not of mutual hostility and suspicion, one will inevitably find difficult border-line cases. And in such cases, I see no test-related substitute for the exercise of legal judgment. That judgment is not a personal judgment. Rather, as in all constitutional cases, it must reflect and remain faithful to the underlying purposes of the Clauses, and it must take account of context and consequences measured in light of those purposes. [The] case before us is a borderline case. [On] the one hand, the Commandments' text undeniably has a religious message, invoking, indeed emphasizing, the Diety. On the other hand, focusing on the text of the Commandments alone cannot conclusively resolve this case. Rather, to determine the message that the text here conveys, we must examine how the text is used. And that inquiry requires us to consider the context of the display.

In certain contexts, a display of the tablets of the Ten Commandments can convey not simply a religious message but also a secular moral message (about proper standards of social conduct). And in certain contexts, a display of the tablets can also convey a historical message (about a historic relation between those standards and the law)—a fact that helps to explain the display of those tablets in dozens of courthouses throughout the Nation, including the Supreme Court of the United States. Here the tablets have been used as part of a display that communicates not simply a religious message, but a secular message as well. The circumstances surrounding the display's placement on the capitol grounds and its physical setting suggest that the State itself intended the latter, nonreligious aspects of the tablets' message to predominate. And the monument's 40–year history on the Texas state grounds indicates that that has been its effect.

The group that donated the monument, the Fraternal Order of Eagles, a private civic (and primarily secular) organization, while interested in the religious aspect of the Ten Commandments, sought to highlight the Commandments' role in shaping civic morality as part of that organization's efforts to combat juvenile delinquency. [The] physical setting of the monument, moreover, suggests little or nothing of the sacred. The monument sits in a large park containing 17 monuments and 21 historical markers, all designed to illustrate the "ideals" of those who settled in Texas and of those who have lived there since that time. [If] these factors provide a strong, but not conclusive, indication that the Commandments' text on this monument conveys a predominantly secular message, a further factor is determinative here. As far as I can tell, 40 years passed in which the presence of this monument, legally speaking, went unchallenged (until the single legal objection raised by petitioner). [Those] 40 years suggest more strongly than can any set of formulaic tests [that] the public visiting the capitol grounds has considered the religious aspect of the tablets' message as part of what is a broader moral and historical message reflective of a cultural heritage.

This case, moreover, is distinguishable from instances where the Court has found Ten Commandments displays impermissible. The display is not on the grounds of a public school, where, given the impressionability of the young, government must exercise particular care in separating church and state. This case also differs from McCreary County, where the short (and stormy) history of the courthouse Commandments' displays demonstrates the substantially religious objectives of those who mounted them, and the effect of this readily apparent objective upon those who view them. That history there indicates a governmental effort substantially to promote religion, not simply an effort primarily to reflect, historically, the secular impact of a religiously inspired document. And, in today's world, in a Nation of so many different religious and comparable nonreligious fundamental beliefs, a more contemporary state effort to focus attention upon a religious text is certainly likely to prove divisive in a way that this longstanding, pre-existing monument has not.

[At] the same time, to reach a contrary conclusion here, based primarily upon on the religious nature of the tablets' text would, I fear, lead the law to exhibit a hostility toward religion that has no place in our Establishment Clause traditions. Such a holding might well encourage disputes concerning the removal of longstanding depictions of the Ten Commandments from public buildings across the Nation. And it could thereby create the very kind of religiously based divisiveness that the Establishment Clause seeks to avoid.

[In] light of these considerations, I cannot agree with today's plurality's analysis. Nor can I agree with Justice Scalia's dissent in McCreary County. I do agree with Justice O'Connor's statement of principles in McCreary County, though I disagree with her evaluation of the evidence as it bears on the application of those principles to this case.

Justice STEVENS, with whom Justice GINSBURG joins, dissenting.

The sole function of the monument on the grounds of Texas' State Capitol is to display the full text of one version of the Ten Commandments. The monument is not a work of art and does not refer to any event in the history of the State. It is significant because, and only because, it communicates the following message: "I AM the LORD thy God. Thou shalt have no other gods before me. Thou shalt not make to thyself any graven images. Thou shalt not take the Name of the Lord thy God in vain. Remember the Sabbath day, to keep it holy. Honor thy father and thy mother, that thy days may be long upon the land which the Lord thy God giveth thee. Thou shalt not kill. Thou shalt not commit adultery. Thou shalt not steal. Thou shalt not bear false witness against thy neighbor. Thou shalt not covet thy neighbor's house. Thou shalt not covet thy neighbor's wife, nor his manservant, nor his maidservant, nor his cattle, nor anything that is thy neighbor's."

Viewed on its face, Texas' display has no purported connection to God's role in the formation of Texas or the founding of our Nation; nor does it provide the reasonable observer with any basis to guess that it was erected to honor any individual or organization. The message transmitted by Texas' chosen display is quite plain: This State endorses the divine code of the "Judeo–Christian" God. [If] any fragment of Jefferson's metaphorical "wall of separation between church and State" is to be preserved, [a] negative answer to that question is mandatory.

I.   [At] the very least, the Establishment Clause has created a strong presumption against the display of religious symbols on public property. [Government's] obligation to avoid divisiveness and exclusion in the religious sphere is compelled by the Establishment and Free Exercise Clauses, which together erect a wall of separation between church and state. [The] wall that separates the church from the State does not prohibit the government from acknowledging the religious beliefs and practices of the American people, nor does it require governments to hide works of art or historic memorabilia from public view just because they also have religious significance. This case, however, is not about historic preservation or the mere recognition of religion. The monolith displayed on Texas Capitol grounds cannot be discounted as a passive acknowledgment of religion, nor can the State's refusal to remove it upon objection be explained as a simple desire to preserve a historic relic. This Nation's resolute commitment to neutrality with respect to religion is flatly inconsistent with the plurality's wholehearted validation of an official state endorsement of the message that there is one, and only one, God.

II.   When the Ten Commandments monument was donated to the State of Texas in 1961, it was not for the purpose of commemorating a noteworthy event in Texas history, signifying the Commandments' influence on the development of secular law, or even denoting the religious beliefs of Texans at that time. To the contrary, the donation was only one of over a hundred largely identical monoliths, and of over a thousand paper replicas, distributed to state and local governments throughout the Nation over the course of several decades. This ambitious project was the work of the Fraternal Order of Eagles, a well-respected benevolent organization whose good works [including combating juvenile delinquency] have earned the praise of several Presidents. [When] Cecil B. DeMille, who at that time was filming the movie The Ten Commandments, heard of [this] endeavor, he teamed up with the Eagles to produce the type of granite monolith now displayed in front of the Texas Capitol and at courthouse squares, city halls, and public parks throughout the Nation.

[Though] the State of Texas may genuinely wish to combat juvenile delinquency, and may rightly want to honor the Eagles for their efforts, it cannot effectuate these admirable purposes through an explicitly religious medium. The State may admonish its citizens not to lie, cheat or steal, to honor their parents and to respect their neighbors' property; and it may do so by printed words, in television commercials, or on granite monuments in front of its public buildings. [The] message at issue in this case, however, is fundamentally different from either a bland admonition to observe generally accepted rules of behavior or a general history lesson.

The reason this message stands apart is that the Decalogue is a venerable religious text. [For] many followers, the Commandments represent the literal word of God as spoken to Moses and repeated to his followers after descending from Mount Sinai. The message conveyed by the Ten Commandments thus cannot be analogized to an appendage to a common article of commerce ("In God we Trust") or an incidental part of a familiar recital ("God save the United States and this honorable Court"). Thankfully, the plurality does not attempt to minimize the religious significance of the Ten Commandments. Attempts to secularize what is unquestionably a sacred text defy credibility and disserve people of faith.

[Moreover,] the Ten Commandments display projects not just a religious, but an inherently sectarian message. There are many distinctive versions of the Decalogue, ascribed to by different religions and even different denominations within a particular faith; to a pious and learned observer, these differences may be of enormous religious significance. In choosing to display this version of the Commandments, Texas tells the observer that the State supports this side of the doctrinal religious debate. [Even] if, however, the message of the monument, despite the inscribed text, fairly could be said to represent the belief system of all Judeo–Christians, it would still run afoul of the Establishment Clause by prescribing a compelled code of conduct from one God, namely a Judeo–Christian God, that is rejected by prominent polytheistic sects, such as Hinduism, as well as nontheistic religions, such as Buddhism. [Today] there are many Texans who do not believe in the God whose Commandments are displayed at their seat of government. Many of them worship a different god or no god at all. Some may believe that the account of the creation in the Book of Genesis is less reliable than the views of men like Darwin and Einstein. [Recognizing] the diversity of religious and secular beliefs held by Texans and by all Americans, it seems beyond peradventure that allowing the seat of government to serve as a stage for the propagation of an unmistakably Judeo–

Christian message of piety would have the tendency to make nonmonotheists and nonbelievers "feel like [outsiders] in matters of faith, and [strangers] in the political community." Pinette.

III.   The plurality relies heavily on the fact that our Republic was founded, and has been governed since its nascence, by leaders who spoke then (and speak still) in plainly religious rhetoric. [The] speeches and rhetoric characteristic of the founding era, however, do not answer the question before us. [When] public officials deliver public speeches, we recognize that their words are not exclusively a transmission from the government because those oratories have embedded within them the inherently personal views of the speaker as an individual member of the polity. The permanent placement of a textual religious display on state property is different in kind; it amalgamates otherwise discordant individual views into a collective statement of government approval.

The plurality's reliance on early religious statements and proclamations made by the Founders is also problematic because those views were not espoused at the Constitutional Convention in 1787 nor enshrined in the Constitution's text. Thus, the presentation of these religious statements as a unified historical narrative is bound to paint a misleading picture. [Notably] absent from their historical snapshot is the fact that Thomas Jefferson refused to issue the Thanksgiving proclamations that Washington had so readily embraced [and] Madison more than once [stated] unequivocally that with respect to government's involvement with religion, the " 'tendency to a usurpation on one side, or the other, or to a corrupting coalition or alliance between them, will be best guarded against by an entire abstinence of the Government from interference, in any way whatever, beyond the necessity of preserving public order, & protecting each sect against trespasses on its legal rights by others.' " These seemingly nonconforming sentiments should come as no surprise. Not insignificant numbers of colonists came to this country with memories of religious persecution by monarchs on the other side of the Atlantic.

[Many] of the Framers understood the word "religion" in the Establishment Clause to encompass only the various sects of Christianity. [For] nearly a century after the Founding, many accepted the idea that America was not just a religious nation, but "a Christian nation." Church of Holy Trinity v. United States, 143 U.S. 457 (1892). The original understanding of the type of "religion" that qualified for constitutional protection under the Establishment Clause likely did not include those followers of Judaism and Islam who are among the preferred "monotheistic" religions Justice Scalia has embraced in his McCreary County opinion. The inclusion of Jews and Muslims inside the category of constitutionally favored religions surely would have shocked Chief Justice Marshall and Justice Story. [Justice Scalia's] inclusion of Judaism and Islam is a laudable act of religious tolerance, but it is one that is unmoored from the Constitution's history and text, and moreover one that is patently arbitrary in its inclusion of some, but exclusion of other (e.g., Buddhism), widely practiced non-Christian religions. [Such a] reading of the First Amendment [would] eviscerate the heart of the Establishment Clause. It would replace Jefferson's "wall of separation" with a perverse wall of exclusion—Christians inside, non-Christians out. It would permit States to construct walls of their own choosing—Baptists inside, Mormons out; Jewish Orthodox inside, Jewish Reform out. A Clause so understood might be faithful to the expectations of some of our Founders, but it is plainly not worthy of a society whose enviable hallmark over the course of two centuries has been the continuing expansion of religious pluralism and tolerance.

[It] is our duty, therefore, to interpret the First Amendment's command that "Congress shall make no law respecting an establishment of religion" not by merely asking what those words meant to observers at the time of the founding, but instead by deriving from the Clause's text and history the broad principles that remain valid today. [The] principle that guides my analysis is neutrality. The basis for that principle is firmly rooted in our Nation's history and our Constitution's text. I recognize that the requirement that government must remain neutral between religion and irreligion would have seemed foreign to some of the Framers. [Fortunately,] we are not bound by the Framers' expectations—we are bound by the legal principles they enshrined in our Constitution. The Establishment Clause [forbids] Texas from displaying the Ten Commandments monument.

Justice O'CONNOR, dissenting.

For essentially the reasons given by Justice Souter, as well as the reasons given in my concurrence in McCreary County, I respectfully dissent.

Justice SOUTER, with whom Justices STEVENS and GINSBURG join, dissenting.

[A] governmental display of an obviously religious text cannot be squared with neutrality, except in a setting that plausibly indicates that the statement is not placed in view with a predominant purpose on the part of government either to adopt the religious message or to urge its acceptance by others. [A] pedestrian happening upon the monument at issue here needs no training in religious doctrine to realize that the statement of the Commandments, quoting God himself, proclaims that the will of the divine being is the source of obligation to obey the rules. [To] ensure that the religious nature of the monument is clear to even the most casual passerby, the word "Lord" appears in all capital letters (as does the word "am"), so that the most eye-catching segment of the quotation is the declaration "I AM the LORD thy God." [Nothing] on the monument [detracts] from its religious nature. [The] government of Texas is telling everyone who sees the monument to live up to a moral code because God requires it, with both code and conception of God being rightly understood as the inheritances specifically of Jews and Christians.

The monument's presentation of the Commandments with religious text emphasized and enhanced stands in contrast to any number of perfectly constitutional depictions of them, the frieze of our own Courtroom providing a good example, where the figure of Moses stands among history's great lawgivers. While Moses holds the tablets of the Commandments showing some Hebrew text, no one looking at the lines of figures in marble relief is likely to see a religious purpose behind the assemblage or take away a religious message from it. Only one other depiction represents a religious leader, and the historical personages are mixed with symbols of moral and intellectual abstractions like Equity and Authority. Since Moses enjoys no especial prominence on the frieze, viewers can readily take him to be there as a lawgiver in the company of other lawgivers.

[Texas] says that the Capitol grounds are like a museum for a collection of exhibits. [The] Government of the United States does not violate the Establishment Clause by hanging Giotto's Madonna on the wall of the National Gallery. But 17 monuments with no common appearance, history, or esthetic role scattered over 22 acres is not a museum, and anyone strolling around the lawn would surely take each memorial on its own terms without any dawning sense that some purpose held the miscellany together more coherently than fortuity and the edge of the grass. One monument expresses admiration for pioneer women. One pays respect to the fighters of World War II. And one quotes the God of Abraham whose command is the sanction for moral law. The themes are individual grit, patriotic courage, and God as the source of Jewish and Christian morality; there is no common denominator.

[Our] numerous prior discussions of Stone have never treated its holding as restricted to the classroom. Nor can the plurality deflect Stone by calling the Texas monument "a far more passive use of [the Decalogue] than was the case in Stone, where the text confronted elementary school students every day." Placing a monument on the ground is not more "passive" than hanging a sheet of paper on a wall when both contain the same text to be read by anyone who looks at it. The problem in Stone was simply that the State was putting the Commandments there to be seen, just as the monument's inscription is there for those who walk by it. To be sure, Kentucky's compulsory-education law meant that the schoolchildren were forced to see the display every day, whereas many see the monument by choice, and those who customarily walk the Capitol grounds can presumably avoid it if they choose. But in my judgment (and under our often inexact Establishment Clause jurisprudence, such matters often boil down to judgment), this distinction should make no difference. The monument in this case sits on the grounds of the Texas State Capitol. There is something significant in the common term "statehouse" to refer to a state capitol building: it is the civic home of every one of the State's citizens. If neutrality in religion means something, any citizen should be able to visit that civic home without having to confront religious expressions clearly meant to convey an official religious position that may be at odds with his own religion, or with rejection of religion.

Page 1610.   Add at end of Note 2:

In CUTTER v. WILKINSON, ___ U.S. ___, 125 S.Ct. 2113 (2005), the Court rejected an Establishment Clause defense raised by prison officials against prisoners' attempts to enforce section 3 of the Religious Land Use and Institutionalized Persons Act of 2000 (RLUIPA), which provides: "No government shall impose a substantial burden on the religious exercise of a person residing in or confined to an institution," unless the burden furthers "a compelling governmental interest," and does so by "the least restrictive means." Congress enacted the statute in reaction to the Court's ruling in Employment Division v. Smith [15th ed., p. 1533], which held that Free Exercise did not require religious exemptions from generally applicable laws, and to the Court's invalidation in City of Boerne v. Flores [15th ed., p. 962], as exceeding Congress's civil rights enforcement authority, of the Religious Freedom Restoration Act, which had attempted to correct Smith by providing statutory religious exemptions across the board.

In Cutter, the Court held unanimously that that the much narrower exemption provisions of RLUIPA on their face qualified as a permissible accommodation of religion. Justice GINSBURG wrote the opinion the Court: "Just last Term, in Locke v. Davey (2004) [15th ed., p. 1519], the Court reaffirmed that 'there is room for play in the joints between' the Free Exercise and Establishment Clauses, allowing the government to accommodate religion beyond free exercise requirements, without offense to the Establishment Clause. [We] hold that § 3 of RLUIPA fits within the corridor between the Religion Clauses: On its face, the Act qualifies as a permissible legislative accommodation of religion that is not barred by the Establishment Clause. Foremost, we find RLUIPA's institutionalized-persons provision compatible with the Establishment Clause because it alleviates exceptional government-created burdens on private religious exercise. Kiryas Joel, Amos. Furthermore, the Act on its face does not founder on shoals our prior decisions have identified: Properly applying RLUIPA, courts must take adequate account of the burdens a requested accommodation may impose on nonbeneficiaries, see Thornton, and they must be satisfied that the Act's prescriptions are and will be administered neutrally among different faiths, see Kiryas Joel. [RLUIPA] protects institutionalized persons who are unable freely to attend to their religious needs and are therefore dependent on the government's permission and accommodation for exercise of their religion.

"We do not read RLUIPA to elevate accommodation of religious observances over an institution's need to maintain order and safety. Our decisions indicate that an accommodation must be measured so that it does not override other significant interests. [We] have no cause to believe that RLUIPA would not be applied in an appropriately balanced way, with particular sensitivity to security concerns. [Lawmakers] supporting RLUIPA were mindful of the urgency of discipline, order, safety, and security in penal institutions. They anticipated that courts would apply the Act's standard with 'due deference to the experience and expertise of prison and jail administrators in establishing necessary regulations and procedures to maintain good order, security and discipline, consistent with consideration of costs and limited resources.' [Should] inmate requests for religious accommodations become excessive, impose unjustified burdens on other institutionalized persons, or jeopardize the effective functioning of an institution, the facility would be free to resist the imposition. In that event, adjudication in as-applied challenges would be in order." Justice THOMAS filed a concurrence reiterating his position that the Establishment Clause is best interpreted in accord with its original meaning as a federalism provision limiting Congress's but not the states' choices of religious policy.

†